Temperament Tools

Working with Your Child's Inborn Traits

REVISED EDITION

Helen Neville, B.S, R.N.
with Diane Clark Johnson, C.F.L.E.

Parenting Press
Chicago

Printed in the United States of America
ISBN 978-1-936903-25-2 paperback

Designed by Magrit Baurecht

Library of Congress Cataloguing-in-Publication Data
available from the publisher

Parenting Press, Inc.
An imprint of Chicago Review Press Incorporated
814 North Franklin Street
Chicago, Illinois 60610

*Book distribution through Independent Publishers Group at www.ipgbook.com and
800-888-4741*

Contents

We dedicate this book—

to our children, who continue to teach us about parenting,

to Jim Cameron, Ph.D., for his generous guidance,

and to our supportive spouses, John and Rob.

Foreword

With a bit of imagination, children can be compared to roads. Some are easy: flat, wide, straight lanes with comfortable, gradual turns and ample shoulders. Others have steep hills, sharp curves, unexpected pot holes, sudden entrances and exits, and no shoulders.

When your child is born, how do you know whether you are going to have a relaxed drive along an easy road or a hair-raising ride down a steep hill?

We once believed that all children were basically the same at birth. One map served as a guide to all children. Now we know that different children develop along different routes, depending on their temperament or behavioral style. Thus parents need more accurate maps to follow their children and plan how to ease the way through some of the difficult spots.

First, you need a clear picture of your child's temperament. Second, with that picture in mind, you need an accurate map to tell you what roadblocks may lie ahead for *your* child. Third, you need a set of guideposts to help navigate those potential roadblocks. Finally, you need to know something about your own temperament and preferred parenting style, so you can pick among the guideposts to find an approach that fits *you*.

From years of temperament counseling with parents, both individually and in groups, Helen F. Neville and Diane Clark Johnson have developed the tools you may need. This book will help you select the individual tools that will work best for you as you pick up that map and travel along the parenting highway with your child.

~ *James Cameron, Ph.D.*
The Preventive Ounce
Oakland, California

Gifts from Birth, Inborn Traits

Most parents now know that children are different from birth. Not so long ago, researchers believed all children were born the same, but turned out differently because of how they were raised. We now know that outcome depends on both nature and nurture—parenting, education, and community. Children differ from birth, and *they remain different.* The goal of this book is to help you understand and bring out the best of your child's inborn temperament.

Pioneering researchers, Stella Chess, M.D., and Alexander Thomas, M.D., identified inborn traits that affect how babies take in and respond to the world. Temperament has since been studied around the world. Children everywhere are born with the same traits, even though cultures may appreciate and support different ones.

Temperament is responsible for many different behaviors. Some babies are very sensitive to clothing textures, flavors, and temperature. Some toddlers are very persistent. Children may be high or low in energy; they may have intense or mellow emotions.

Understanding temperament makes your job easier. Imagine that your new baby is like a mysterious island. A map would help! Temperament is the map that makes exploring easier and more enjoyable. When you know what to expect, you can travel with more confidence.

James Cameron, Ph.D., continued the work of researchers Chess and Thomas. He studied hundreds of temperament evaluations and found that children with similar traits often have similar behavior issues. He then explored temperament-based management tools. His work is the basis of this book.

Understanding temperament can prevent many behavior problems because parents can work *with* rather than *against* inborn traits. When parenting style and environment fit with temperament, children can thrive and grow.

How can you tell if behavior is due to temperament or something else? Ask yourself, "When did this behavior begin?" If it goes *way* back, it's likely related to temperament. If it just started a few days (weeks or months) ago, it's more likely due to illness, a step in development, or a reaction to personal, family, or social stress.

Understanding temperament helps avoid unnecessary blame and guilt. Though there are no bad traits, some take more work. With practice, parents can learn to appreciate and work with their child's traits. *They learn not to blame* children for their temperament.

It takes more skill to manage an airplane than a bicycle, and more skill and effort to manage a spirited child than a mellow one. Parents need not feel guilty when they have a harder time. Those who criticize often have easy children, and mistakenly believe their ease is due to their parenting ability.

Are traits good or bad? No. Just as bicycles, cars, and airplanes each have their own pros and cons, so it is with temperament. Sometimes it's better to be very curious, sometimes very cautious. Sometimes it's helpful to be very flexible and at others very determined. The goal is to discover where and how one's traits are valuable.

How does temperament relate to personality? Personality is like a layer cake. The bottom layer, temperament, is there at the beginning. Other layers get added: growth and development, relationships with family, friends, health, school, community, and all the adventures of life. Temperament affects how each child takes in and reacts to each new layer. Over time, because of inborn temperament, children are attracted to different experiences in life. This book is about the powerful bottom layer, *temperament.*

Does temperament change over time? Some inborn traits continue. Active babies usually become active adults. Emotional intensity generally remains high or low, as it was in the beginning. Over time, children can learn to *manage* their traits more effectively: the intense child learns to use words rather than hit and bite. Experience is also important. Many toddlers who are cautious or shy around new people and places are much less so by elementary school. This is simply because much more of the world is already familiar. Caution may reappear when future life changes come along.

What Makes My Child Tick?

Parents generally know their children better than anyone else. Fill in the temperament chart below by thinking carefully about your baby or young child. One baby always cried and arched her back in her infant seat. Her twin sat wide-eyed and still in his seat, causing the pediatrician to remark, "Some babies soak up the world with their eyes." If you have more than one child, you may have seen such differences soon after birth. However, many babies need the first few months to settle in, so their true temperament is more reliably visible at 4 months.

Temperament Chart

For each of the traits, read the descriptions and consider whether your child's temperament falls at one extreme or another or is somewhere in the middle. Many children are middle of the road in most traits, but may be extreme in one or two. More rarely (and more challengingly), some are extreme in several, or most, traits. Notice that there are extremes at each end of each temperament line. Sometimes it helps to ask your partner, the child's grandparents, a child care provider or teacher, or someone else who knows the child well.

1. Activity

Low energy. This infant relaxes in the infant seat and high chair. He sleeps peacefully. As a toddler he snuggles contentedly on your lap or sits with toys in the center of the room. Arms and legs relax as you dress him. As a preschooler, he usually moves slowly and uses hands more than feet. He manipulates small toys, enjoys art work, puzzles, or building.

High energy. This infant kicked vigorously before birth and likely walked early. Even when asleep, she wiggles across the crib. Arms and legs fly during diaper changes. As a toddler, she hates being imprisoned in high chair or car seat. As a preschooler, she talks fast and moves fast. She loves large spaces for play, dances while watching videos, and wiggles while listening to stories.

Mark your child's activity with an X anywhere along the scale.

Activity
Low energy   High energy

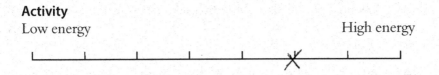

2. Adaptability

High (Flexible). This infant glides comfortably through daily transitions—waking, being picked up, bathed, put down, and falling asleep. As a toddler, she quickly settles into new situations. She drinks milk from breast, bottle, red cup or blue one. As a preschooler, she gets along easily with playmates and goes with the flow when family plans change.

Low (Natural planner). This infant may cry upon waking and going to sleep. His body stiffens when he's picked up or moved and he doesn't like having his face washed. Even as a toddler, he often has a plan in his head, and needs time to switch from one activity to another. He resists getting dressed; he protests if you don't give him the same blue cup at breakfast. He objects to getting in the car and dawdles while getting out. He may be fussy and short tempered in the late afternoon and may have trouble falling asleep. As a preschooler, he complains when plans change or when you cut his toast the wrong way. He bosses playmates around because he wants them to play the game he sees *in his head*.

Mark your child's adaptability level with an X anywhere along the scale.

Adaptability
High (Flexible)   Low (Natural planner)

3. Approach to new things (Curious or Cautious)

Curious. This infant tries out new foods and automatically reaches toward new toys and pets. As a toddler, he immediately climbs into a new bed, smiles at the new baby sitter, or joins a new play group. He's attracted to all new things, whether safe or dangerous. This preschooler is always ready to check out a new friend, a new house, a new park, or a new school.

Cautious. This infant wrinkles her nose at the smell of a new food or spits it out. She turns away or cries when a stranger approaches. She watches others play with a new toy before trying it herself. As a toddler and preschooler, she hides silently behind parents as they greet someone new. She's sure that the old bed, house, or school is better than any new one could be.

Mark your child's approach to new things with an X anywhere along the scale.

Approach to new things

Curious   Cautious

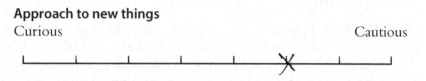

4. Frustration reaction

Children face many frustrations as they learn new things and bump into limits. Some handle frustration easily. Others get quickly discouraged or angry when things don't go their way.

Persistent with learning and patient with limits. Some children persist as they play or practice new things, and they patiently accept limits. This infant patiently waits for milk and later she practices standing or walking despite the tumbles. As a toddler, she entertains herself by trying out a new toy again and again. Her inborn motto is, "If at first you don't succeed, try, try again." If she can't have the TV remote or eat from the dog's dish, she may fuss but quickly accepts another activity. As a preschooler, she happily plays and practices over and over. In the process, she acquires many new skills. The frustration of limits (time at the park is over or bedtime stories are finished) generally slips by easily.

Frustrated by learning and limits. When hungry, this infant yells for milk right now! As a toddler, he goes back again and again to climb on the forbidden coffee table. Discouraged by things that are hard, he browses from one toy to another looking for what's easy. As a preschooler, even necessary limits make him instantly angry. He pushes again and again for a new toy at the store and more time on your smart phone. He throws the blocks that topple over and won't try the scissors today because they didn't work yesterday. He pleads for help getting dressed because it's *too hard* to do by himself. He loves videos because success is guaranteed.

At first, it seems confusing that these children persist at what parents *don't want* and walk away from what parents do want. Their goal is to *avoid* frustration. They escape the frustration of *accepting* limits by pushing past them whenever they can. With play and learning, they avoid discouragement and fear of failure by walking away.

Mark your child's frustration reaction with an X anywhere along the scale.

Frustration reaction
Persistent with learning & patient with limits
Frustrated by learning and limits

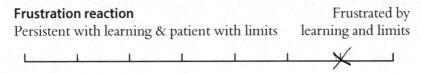

5. Intensity of emotions

Mellow. This infant silently smiles his joy or frowns his distress. As a toddler, his body remains relaxed even as emotions parade across his face. As a preschooler, he can stand quietly and tell his playmate that his feelings were hurt. Strong feelings are rare and quickly fade back into calmness.

Dramatic. This infant squeals with pleasure or screams with distress. As a toddler, she may bite when she's happy or angry. She loves or hates bright lights, dressing, bath time, each toy and person. She expresses feelings with her whole body. When she's upset, everyone knows it! As a preschooler, she reacts strongly to excitement, praise, criticism, or disappointment. She may smack a playmate before calming down enough to use her words. There are no small feelings. Everything is fabulous or horrible.

Mark your child's emotional intensity with an X anywhere along the scale.

Intensity of emotions
Mellow
Dramatic

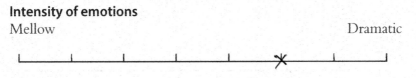

6. Mood

Sunny/Easy to soothe. This baby wakes with a smile and settles to sleep with a contented sigh. She smiles on the changing table, in your arms, and at strangers. When distress comes along, she quickly settles back to her sunny self. Throughout childhood, she is generally easy to soothe or distract out of distress and disappointments.

Somber/Hard to soothe. This infant gets upset more often and takes longer to calm down. He fusses when things aren't "just so." Other temperament traits feed into this one. For example, the toddler who is highly sensitive or easily frustrated feels many more upsets each day. If he's also intense, those are all *big* upsets rather than little ones. And if he is slow to adapt, it's hard to pull out of an emotional pit once he's in one. As a preschooler, his world view may incline toward "My glass is half empty."

Mark your child's mood with an X anywhere along the scale.

Mood
Sunny/Easy to soothe   Somber/Hard to soothe

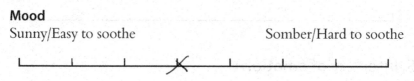

7. Regularity

Predictable. This infant has an internal alarm clock—he wakes and gets hungry and tired at the same times each day. As a toddler, he's automatically on schedule. You can predict when he'll be most active each day and when tomorrow's poop will come. Because he's sleepy at the same time each night, it's easy to establish a bedtime routine that works like a charm.

Irregular. One day this infant wakes early, the next day she sleeps late. She takes long naps or short naps. There's no predicting her schedule. As a toddler, she eats three small meals some days and five big ones on others. As a preschooler, she may get grouchy because no one expected her to need food or rest at that time. She's not sleepy at the same hour each night.

Mark your child's regularity with an X anywhere along the scale.

Regularity
Predictable   Irregular

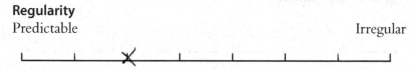

8. Sensitivity

Low. This infant sleeps through parties and plane rides. One brand of food tastes the same as another, and a polyester shirt feels the same as pure cotton. This toddler may ignore the scratch on her knee, the dull ache in her ear, or the load in her diaper. As a preschooler, she may not particularly notice the emotions of other people.

High. This infant wakes with small noises or sudden light. He notices gentle touch, temperature, textures, and smells. This toddler notices your new glasses or haircut. A dry diaper feels different from a wet one.

His ear may be uncomfortable before the doctor can see any sign of an ear infection. He gets overwhelmed with too much noise, light, or excitement. As a preschooler, he notices tiny sounds and faint smells. He reads others' emotions easily and may react to even mild approval and disapproval.

Mark your child's sensitivity with an X anywhere along the scale.

Sensitivity
Low   High

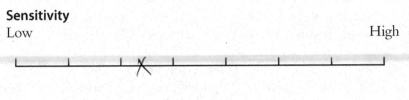

Summary

You may want to copy the scores above onto the temperament poster on page 16 so you can get an overview of your child's temperament. In general (not always), the more the marks fall toward the middle or the left, the easier the parent's job. In general, the more the marks fall to the far right, the more challenging the parent's job.

Without intending to, parents can increase their child's distress by pushing *against* his temperament rather than working *with* it. A goal of this book is to help you work toward creating "good fit" between your child and his environment. Then his life will be easier and so will yours.

In considering your child's temperament, it's important to take the long view. The persistence that wears you down may later be used to make the world a better place. The drama that seems unnecessary to you may be the charismatic attraction of a future leader. The energy that tires you will be an asset in athletics. There are positive sides to every position on the temperament scales.

Your child may be different from what you expected and unique in ways you didn't anticipate. If you hoped for a dramatic artist and got instead an introspective scholar (or vice versa), you'll be wise to substitute a dream more appropriate to your child's temperament.

Behavior that Goes with Temperament Clusters

As mentioned earlier, Dr. Cameron mapped out behavior issues that commonly occur with different clusters of temperament traits. One way to discover what makes your child tick is to read the behavior lists below. Which list best matches the issues you face with your child?

There is a page number after each cluster. You can go directly to that chapter, or you may prefer to read chapter 3 first (page 17).

The baby or child of *moderate temperament* generally eats, sleeps, and accepts limits fairly easily. In many ways, this is an "easy" child, though there will be ups and downs with stages of development. If your child doesn't fit any of the following clusters, come back to this one. See page 25.

The *flexible, low energy* child calmly looks for something else if a playmate snatches his toy. When friends announce, "Let's go build with the blocks!" this child climbs out of the sandbox to comply. Not being assertive, others may take advantage of his agreeable nature. See page 32.

The *low energy, easily discouraged* child dawdles, depends on parents, and resists separation. Such children seem so clingy and fragile that parents wonder if they will ever leave home. See page 35.

The *sensitive, intense, cautious* child refuses to eat new foods or join new activities. May bite or hit when stressed. Has difficulty leaving parents. Parents worry that he'll never make friends, have a life of his own, or eat a well-balanced diet. May be high or low in energy. See page 42.

The child who is a *strong-willed perfectionist* wants everything "just so." Is often too excited to get to sleep and may wake repeatedly. Has trouble leaving parents. Feelings get hurt easily. Has long, loud, or frequent temper tantrums: argues, bites, hits. May hold breath, vomit, or bang head when upset. Visits to the doctor are difficult. May be high or low in energy, See page 49.

The *active, slow to adapt* child doesn't like to cuddle and demands to feed herself. Moving full-steam on her own course, she talks constantly and bosses her friends around. Adapting to life can wear her out and lead to meltdowns late in the day. Trips can be terribly difficult. See page 59.

The *fast-moving, easily frustrated* child won't sit still to eat, dashes away from parents, often demands help and then refuses it. Has temper tantrums and a short attention span. Quickly becomes bored so has an eye for trouble; may be the class clown or blame others unfairly. Can have trouble getting along with friends. See page 68.

The ***active, intense, easily frustrated, slow to adapt*** child is so often unhappy or out of control that you feel worried, frightened, or overwhelmed. You work harder than other parents to be consistent and patient. Nonetheless, life with your child is still very difficult. Start on page 86.

Which list above shows the issues you struggle with the most? Some children fit more than one temperament cluster, so are described in several chapters. Each succeeding chapter represents a more challenging child. Follow the page numbers to find the most helpful chapter. In it, you will find the tools that will be especially useful to you and your child.

   If your child has a generally moderate temperament, but is extreme in one trait, you will find help in chapter 4, pp. 25–31.

Note: Parents in this book are referred to as Mom and Dad. However, whether you are a traditional couple, single parent, grandparent or other relative, or same sex couple, you will find many tools here for working with temperament. Explore what works for *your* child.

Temperament Poster

Copy this chart, and fill it in for all family members. Post it where you can refer to it easily and often as you make parenting decisions—on the refrigerator, the bedroom door, the car dashboard, etc.

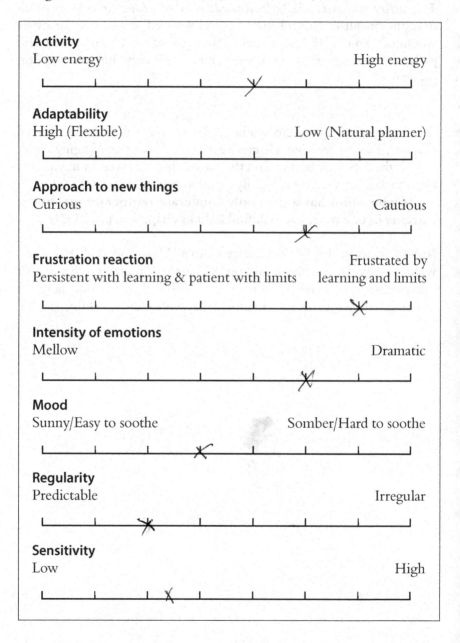

Activity
Low energy   High energy

Adaptability
High (Flexible)   Low (Natural planner)

Approach to new things
Curious   Cautious

Frustration reaction
Persistent with learning & patient with limits   Frustrated by learning and limits

Intensity of emotions
Mellow   Dramatic

Mood
Sunny/Easy to soothe   Somber/Hard to soothe

Regularity
Predictable   Irregular

Sensitivity
Low   High

❸

Temperament Tango, Parent & Child Together

An important part of understanding behavior is how the parents' and the child's temperaments interact. On the temperament chart you filled in for your child, mark your position on each of the temperament traits.

As you look at some traits, you may feel a significant difference between your "natural" self and how you currently live your life. If so, mark "I" for inborn and "C" for current. As noted earlier, some traits may shift over time.

Sometimes life is easier when you share your child's traits, and sometimes it's easier when you are opposites. This chapter highlights common interactions between parent and child, based on the charts you filled in for each. Find the traits below where either you or your child is high or low and read what you can do to improve your relationship.

1. Activity

Both child and parent are low energy

You share quiet, slower paced activities. Few problems arise.

- *For your health, exercise together gently. Go for walks together.*
- *Encourage exercise with younger children. Your child may feel more competent than with age-mates who are active or athletically gifted.*

Child, low energy | Parent, high energy

To you, your child seems lazy. She tires quickly and doesn't like sports. She is unlikely to excel in athletics.

- *Respect her slower pace.*
- *Listen to people who point out her other special abilities.*
- *Jog while you push her stroller or jog around the sandbox she's playing quietly in.*
- *Get child care so you can go out for the exercise you need.*

• • • • •

Both child and parent are high energy

You understand this child's need to move. One active 3-year-old could jog a mile with his six-foot father. Of course, even active parents can get worn out by active children!

○ *Enjoy being active with your child.*
○ *Remember to slow down before you or your child is overtired.*

Child, high energy | Parent, low energy

Think of a time when you *really* needed to get to the bathroom. Remember how your body demanded that you move? Imagine your body always being that anxious to get somewhere. That's how your child feels.

○ *Remind yourself that your child needs to move as much as you need to rest or do quiet activities.*
○ *Arrange part of your house to be safe for active play with wheel toys, bouncy horse, balls to throw, bed or cushions to jump on, etc.*
○ *Find safe, fenced playgrounds.*
○ *Line up active relatives, sitters, other children, and child care workers who match your child's energy level.*
○ *Use a harness (rather than a stroller) so your toddler can exercise safely.*

2. Adaptability

Both child and parent are slow to adapt (natural planners)

Life would be easier with a more adaptable (flexible) child. You are both low in adaptability, but you are the mature adult. That puts the burden to adapt on you.

○ *Establish routines that you both can live with. Planning ahead makes life easier.*
○ *Keep in touch with parents of older children. Then when your child reaches a new developmental stage, you'll feel better prepared.*

Both child and parent are highly flexible

Living together is relatively easy because you both go with the flow. Few problems arise.

• • • • •

Child, low (natural planner) | Parent, highly flexible

You adjust more easily than your child. The problem with this is that you may eventually become resentful because you feel like you give in all the time. For example, your child wants you to snuggle until she falls asleep. How long are you genuinely willing to stay with her?

- *Hold the line on things that are personally important to you, which may mean snuggling for 15 minutes, no longer.*
- *Set aside time to take care of your needs.*
- *Be kind and consistent, knowing that your child will adjust in time.*

Child, highly flexible | Parent, low (natural planner)

Your flexible child may adapt quickly to your more settled ways. However, if he has to do all the adapting, he may become resentful.

- *As a responsive parent, push yourself to adapt to your child as well.*

3. Approach to new things

Both child and parent are curious

You and your child are both attracted to all that is new and different.

- *Model exploring safely. For example, there is a strange dog nearby. Talk to its owner to find out if it's friendly before petting it. Invite your child to notice if the dog's tail is wagging (friendly), or whether its ears are laid back (not friendly or perhaps scared).*

Both child and parent are cautious

If you are or were painfully cautious and shy, you want your child to feel more comfortable.

- *Prepare her ahead of time for new experiences.*
- *Know that she needs to study new situations before she steps in.*
- *Help her learn in small steps how to join the group or do a new activity.*
- *Be patient and understanding when she doesn't want to join the crowd or do something new.*
- *Continue to offer new opportunities at a pace that builds her confidence.*

• • • • •

Child, curious | Parent, cautious

This is a hard temperament combination. Either you feel frightened by your child's adventurous spirit, or she feels imprisoned because of your caution.

- *Talk with more adventuresome parents to see how they view your child's behavior before you set limits that may be overly cautious.*
- *Practice imagining this child surrounded by a protective golden light or bubble.*
- *This image will keep you calmer.*

Child, cautious | Parent, curious

When you are naturally adventuresome, it's hard to have a child who is cautious. Imagine visiting Mars tomorrow—you'd be greatly excited and also concerned about safety. Your child feels that concern when at a new slide or in a room of new people.

O *Let him move into new adventures at his own pace. He'll be much more likely to feel courageous if he knows you support him in a sympathetic manner.*

4. Frustration reaction

Both child and parent manage frustration easily

Both you and your child push through difficulty. When projects don't work at first, you both keep going to see them through. When you have a difference of opinion, you're both naturally inclined to keep looking for solutions. Appreciate this valuable trait you share.

Both child and parent quickly upset by frustration

Both you and your child prefer to avoid things that are difficult, annoying, or discouraging. It's harder for you than for other parents to repeatedly enforce necessary rules and to patiently help your child learn.

O *Ask for the help of family, friends, and other parents with children. It is not necessary to do everything alone. Both you and your child will benefit from the care and assistance of others. Create a village!*

• • • • •

Child, manages frustration easily
Parent, quickly upset by frustration

It's harder for you than for other parents to model patience to your child. It's also harder to enforce necessary rules calmly and repeatedly.

O *Pick only one or two important rules to teach at a time. That way, you'll see results sooner and become less discouraged.*

O *Put a check on the calendar each time you enforce a limit. Plan how you might reward yourself when you get five or fifteen checks.*

O *Remind yourself that the harder you work in the beginning to enforce this rule every time, the faster your child will learn.*

Child, quickly upset by frustration
Parent, manages frustration easily

It's hard for you to imagine why your child reacts so differently to frustration. For the child who is easily frustrated, many of life's goals lie at the bottom of a 12-foot swimming pool. During the dive to fetch them, the importance of the goal vanishes. The need for air (for relief from frustration) overpowers motivation so she backs off, either discouraged or angry. She needs a patient parent to help her find a long-handled net, or to drain the pool. Otherwise, she may stick with easy goals that float on the surface and never get to the bigger ones on the bottom.

- *Expect resistance to limits. Choose your battles and use your persistence to calmly enforce necessary limits.*
- *Expect her to back off when the going gets tough. Assume she will need help to follow through. Use your persistence to help her break goals into small, manageable pieces.*
- *Discover her personal strengths and abilities as these will be easier for her to pursue.*

5. Intensity of emotions

Both child and parent are mellow

You make an easy-going, mellow pair!

Both child and parent are intense, dramatic

When you are loud and upset, your child automatically becomes more so. The level of intensity can quickly spiral out of control.

- *When you are upset, stop talking. Take two or three deep breaths before you say another word.*
- *Deliberately speak slowly and quietly. Keep body movements small.*
- *When you can't control your strong feelings, step away from your child and go somewhere else to calm down.*

• • • • •

Child, mellow | Parent, intense, dramatic

Your intensity may unintentionally overpower the feelings of your mellow child. By comparison to yours, her quiet emotions are in danger of seeming insignificant. Consequently, for example, she may learn to hide her excitement so that it isn't swept away in your more intense world. Further, if you are greatly distressed by her discomfort, she may learn not to express it. Kept inside, her own distress is all she has to deal with. Once expressed, she may feel obliged to "take care" of both her original distress and you, her distressed parent. She may learn to conceal pain so there is only one issue for her to manage at a time.

○ *Listen carefully to your child, allowing her to tell you about things in her own way.*

○ *Resist your urge to intensify or add to your child's account.*

○ *When you talk with her about her life, be interested and calm. Contain your excitement and distress so that your intensity doesn't overpower hers.*

○ *Be cautious about how much of your personal life to reveal. Rely on friends, other family members, and therapists for your primary emotional support.*

Child, intense, dramatic | Parent, mellow

Your calm manner helps your child stay calm. Don't be frightened or controlled by her high intensity.

○ *Avoid the urge to say, "It's not a big deal. Get over it!"*

○ *When your child is falling apart, report back to her, "I see (hear) how really upset you are about . . ."*

○ *Later, when things are calm, tell about an occasion when you had similar feelings.*

6. Mood

Regardless of initial inclination in mood, research shows the emotional benefit of practicing gratitude. After reviewing the day's troubles at dinner or at bedtime, lift the mood by taking a few minutes to appreciate things that were pleasant, beautiful, fun, interesting, or enjoyable.

7. Regularity

Both child and parent are regular

You'll work together like the parts of a well-oiled machine!

Both child and parent are irregular

You are both inclined to eat and sleep according to an array of body signals. Such a "hang loose" lifestyle can work well for stay-at-home families until the school years begin. If the child is also low in adaptability, he may be less fussy on a more regular routine so he knows what's coming next.

○ *Start a few weeks before school begins to move into a more regular schedule.*

○ *If needed, provide routine and regularity for a slow to adapt child.*

• • • • •

Child, regular | Parent, irregular

This child's body works on a strong natural clock.

- *Set an alarm clock to remind yourself when to start a meal preparation or begin the bedtime routine.*
- *Adapt to your child's schedule for now. As he becomes more able to take care of himself, you'll be able to go back to your less regular ways.*

Child, irregular | Parent, regular

You're probably used to living by the clock, but your child isn't.

- *Because your child's body is unpredictable, watch her signals to see when she needs to eat and sleep.*
- *Work gradually toward a more regular schedule that will suit you better.*

8. Sensitivity

Both child and parent are low sensitivity

Both you and your child may find it difficult to know how the other feels. Most of the time you get along just fine. Sometimes you may get into arguments that startle you because neither of you knew the other was upset.

- *Ask your child intermittently, "How are you feeling?"*
- *Teach her words to describe her feelings.*
- *Some low sensitivity children don't notice when they are hungry. They just get grouchy. If so, keep healthy snacks within their reach. To avoid power struggles, don't push your child to eat. Instead, invite, "I wonder if you'd feel better if you had a snack."*

Both child and parent are high sensitivity

You have the good fortune to understand where the other is coming from. Be aware that your feelings may easily blend or resonate. When one feels bad, the other may automatically feel guilty.

- *Speak up clearly and specifically when you are annoyed so that painful feelings don't float around unresolved. Teach your child to do the same.*

• • • • •

Child, low sensitivity | Parent, high sensitivity

You live in a world that your child cannot understand. You may feel battered by the noise, commotion, and mess he creates.

- *Accept him as he is and take care of yourself, too. For example, wear earplugs to block out some of his noise instead of nagging him to be quiet.*
- *Decide what areas of the house he can mess up and which he cannot.*

- *Play your favorite music to block out some of the background noise.*
- *Avoid feeling like your child doesn't care about you or anyone else.*
- *Help him notice others' feelings, body language, and tones of voice.*

Child, high sensitivity | Parent, low sensitivity

Your child lives in a very different world than you do—full of sensations that you barely notice.

- *Honor her sensitivity and believe what she tells you about her world and how she feels.*
- *Learn from her how to notice more what others are feeling.*

❹

Pawly Puppy
The Child of Moderate Temperament

Pawly Puppy is the child most parents expect to have: a precious being full of joy and occasional tears. She alternates between excitedly exploring her world and snuggling with Mom or Dad to enjoy her favorite story. Early on, Pawly says what she wants with a look or a pointing finger. As she grows older, her requests come politely or excitedly, seldom unpleasantly. When Mom is busy, she complains, but can wait. When something doesn't work at first, she automatically tries again, and then may ask for help. She learns new rules after just a few repetitions. She usually meets disappointment with a sad face or whining, only occasionally with screaming and tantrums. Pawly Puppy is easy to live with and easy to love.

Keys to Living with the Child of Moderate Temperament

Just because Pawly has a moderate temperament doesn't mean it's easy to be her parent. Pawly needs what all children need:

- **Acceptance of stages of development.** The demanding 2s and feisty 4s are especially full of ups and downs.

- **Support for personal growth.** Pawly needs love and support in expressing her feelings, understanding who she is, and making the best of her abilities.

- **Clarity.** She needs clear, consistent rules, to learn what is expected.

- **Support when her family suffers stress.** Pawly needs her parents to resolve their personal problems in order to be available to her. She needs support during stressful times—new house, new baby, new child care; or poverty, divorce, family illness, or domestic violence.

- **Time.** Despite her parents' busy schedules in a culture that offers precious little support to the essential job of parenting, Pawly needs attention from her parents.

Parent Care

Early on, Pawly's mom got frustrated with other parents who complained, "It's so hard being a parent!" Pawly's mom suggested, "If you'd just be calm and consistent, your child would be calm and cooperative like Pawly." Some parents resented her suggestions. As Pawly's mom learned about inborn temperament, she realized that other children really can be much more difficult. She gradually learned to empathize. She also felt lucky that she had an easy child like Pawly.

Common Behavior Issues

- Discipline, pp. 96–102.
- Sleep, pp. 102–109.

Children with One Extreme Trait

Some children of generally easy temperament have one temperament trait that is extreme. Behavior issues tend to revolve around that single trait. For example, an easy child who is highly active may be easy in all regards except that it takes a great deal of energy to keep up with her. To avoid exhaustion, her parents and care givers need to take turns and rest when she does.

Highlighted below are behavior challenges associated with extremes of each trait. Look for the trait which showed up as extreme on your child's profile. You'll find helpful tools below. The traits are listed in alphabetical order.

Activity, high energy

- **Dependent, clingy.** Very active children are usually outgoing and independent. If your child is not her usual self, she may be getting sick or reacting to family stress. Problems between her parents can change this child's more typically outgoing behavior. After she has been especially excited and on the go for a few days, she may cling tightly for a day or two in order to reconnect with you.

- **Discipline.** See pp. 96–102.

- **Eating.** Around 7 to 8 months, active babies want to be more in charge of mealtime. Some eat quickly and others more slowly. Between one nibble and the next, they want to finger paint with food or drum on the tray with a spoon. Plan to eat your own meal or do kitchen chores while this child eats.

Active children nibble and graze throughout the day. They tend to eat small meals and frequent snacks. Most don't gain too much weight because they burn calories as fast as they eat them, but check with the doctor to be sure. Avoid fights about food. When they drop food from the high chair, you might offer a toy for these physics experiments, or assume the meal is over and put them down.

o **Fearfulness.** Active children may suddenly become more fearful around 9 or 10 months of age. They may be afraid of heights, or noises, or unexpected events. This change may be related to new growth in parts of the brain. Generally, such fearfulness passes in a few weeks.

o **No!** Some high energy children learn "No!" and "Don't!" at 11 or 12 months of age. They may practice this new power tool while being bathed or dressed. They may simply be playing, or "No!" may signal the beginning of new independence, just as walking does. If you have time, go along with your child and let her enjoy her power. If you have a schedule to meet, go ahead and do what you need to do, even if she objects.

o **Standing all the time.** Around 9 or 10 months, when active children first learn to stand, they don't want to sit! They prefer to stand while eating, getting diapers changed, and when in bed. They may wake and stand up during the night, before they know how to sit down again. Fortunately, they soon learn how to sit. At this age, they're more able to cooperate when standing up. They may eat better standing by a low table than when forced to sit in a high chair. This is normal behavior for this temperament. Once standing is no longer so new and exciting, they will sit for short periods. (Tip: Immediately stand your toddler up after the nurse gives a shot. He'll usually feel much better.)

For more help, see:
- Child care/Preschool, pp. 71–72
- Create a village, page 70.
- Friendly with strangers, page 74.
- Impulsiveness, pp. 75–77.
- Sleep, pp. 102–109.

Activity, low energy

○ **Eating.** Some quiet youngsters want to start feeding themselves around 6 months of age. Others wait until long after they are able! Go with the flow on this and avoid struggles about eating.

Adaptability, low

For more help, see:
• Child care/Preschool, page 62.
• Discipline, pp. 96–102.
• Doctor's visits, page 54.
• Separation, pp. 55–56.
• Potty training, pp. 109–112.
• Sleep, pp. 102–109.
• Stubborn, page 56.
• Weaning, page 57.

Adaptability, high

○ **Bumps and bruises.** All children fall while learning to stand. Highly adaptable children may get up and try again without even stopping to cry. Put mats or rugs at their favorite practicing places, or they may silently collect bumps and bruises.

Approach, cautious

○ **Dependence.** Expect these children to become more whiny, clingy, and dependent when they learn new things—learning to walk, starting a new school, or adjusting to a new sibling. Expect two steps forward, one step back. If you push them to be more independent before they are ready, they become more clingy. Independence returns sooner if they get the support and reassurance they need.

For more help, see:
• Tarita Turtle, pp. 35–41.

Approach, curious

○ **Boredom.** These children may become bored quickly once things become familiar. Give lots of safe opportunities to explore. As they reach age 3 or 4, teach safety rules. Do things together so that you can teach them how to do things safely. Rather than say, "Don't ever light matches!" say, "If you want to light matches, tell me and we'll do it together. Always do this with an adult."

o **Gets into everything.** These natural explorers reach out and touch everything—your hair, glasses, lamps, pets, plants, phone, and computer. Childproof the house, yard, and car thoroughly! Keep the grocery cart in the center of the store aisle. If their energy and intensity are moderate, teach them how to touch gently: "Touch it but don't move it." Thus, they can satisfy their curiosity without causing harm. If they are intense and can't control their bodies, encourage them to "Hold your hands behind your back and look."

Frustration reaction, easily frustrated by learning and by limits

o **Tests limits.** When you say, "No cookie before dinner," they may bargain for half a cookie or a quarter or "at least a tiny crumb." When you say, "Stop climbing the fence," they may wait until you look the other way and then try again. They try to push past or around you. Set reasonable limits and stick to them calmly, firmly, and consistently.

For more help, see:
- Frustrated by limits, page 69.
- Frustrated by learning, page 70.
- Lying, page 77.
- Separation, pp. 81–82.
- Sleep, pp. 102–109.

Frustration reaction, persists with learning and patient with limits

o **Keep trying.** These children keep practicing and learning in spite of difficulty. They resist moving on until they finish their building or drawing. For schoolwork and as adults this is a very useful trait. They accept reasonable limits fairly easily.

Intensity of emotions, dramatic

o Friends. Intense children do better in small, low energy groups. Like gasoline poured on a barbecue, large groups of intense children or adults get these children all wound up. Small groups offer more predictability. Invite just one preschooler for a play date. Consider a small home daycare with six children rather than a center with 25.

For more help, see:
- Biting and hitting, pp. 90–91.
- Child care/Preschool, pp. 51–52.
- Discipline, pp. 96–102.
- Sleep, pp. 102–109.

Intensity, mellow

o Lost in the crowd. The mellow feelings of these children are not obvious from the outside. Take time regularly to ask and talk about their feelings. Teach them words to express their feelings and wishes.

Regularity, irregular

o Eating. These children may eat a lot at one meal and not much at the next. If they are hungry at 5 p.m., but not given food, stored sugar is released from their liver to keep them going. So at the 6 p.m. dinnertime, they may *not* be hungry. The solution is to offer small nutritious snacks when they are hungry, as long as they are not gaining weight too fast.

o Sleep. See pp. 102–109.

Regularity, predictable

o Time changes. This child's body runs on its own clock. Expect her to get tired and hungry at the same time every day, including days when your schedule is different (weekend, holidays, crisis days). It takes her longer than other people to adjust to changes in daylight saving time.

Sensitivity, high

o Dependence. Sensitive babies, of average energy level, are often content to let parents give them more help than they really need around 9 to 10 months of age. Thus they may appear more capable with a baby sitter than with Mom and Dad. Give your baby some time to try things for herself before you jump in to help.

o **Strong sensory reactions.** These children are genuinely super sensitive to their environments. Respect this trait even if you do not share it or find it hard to understand. Such children may react strongly to smells and flavors of foods, textures of clothing, temperatures, certain sounds, and light. A few of these babies have extremely sensitive skin. Being gently stroked can feel startling and unpleasant instead of soothing. Hold such a baby with gentle firmness. Think of giving gentle pressure to the muscles *under* the skin, rather than stroking the skin. As these children grow, help them describe and take care of their sensitive bodies.

Sensitivity, low

o **Emotional awareness.** From early on, most sensitive children easily read other people's emotional cues and body language. Help your *less* sensitive preschooler learn the language of emotions. Make faces at each other in the mirror and name the feelings. Talk about the feelings you see in picture books and on videos with the sound turned off.

o **Illness.** Children with low sensitivity are often less aware of body sensations, like the pain of a sore throat or early ear infection. If they are also low in intensity, they tend not to complain. If your child is listless, or out of sorts, or sleeping poorly, or eating less than usual, check for fever or other signs of illness.

o **Potty training.** See pp. 109–112.

5

Cam Chameleon
The Low Energy, Highly
Adaptable Child

Like the amazing chameleon that changes its appearance to match the surroundings, Cam Chameleon blends in so well that it can be hard to see him. Cam is a quiet child. While others run and yell, he plays peacefully in the sandbox. He draws, does puzzles, and builds with blocks. Cam is a parent's delight—mellow, flexible, and easy to get along with. Dinner isn't ready? He waits patiently. Dad's on the phone? He plays by himself. When his favorite bowl needs washing or his friend can't come to play, Cam is content with another bowl and is happy to play with a different friend. Cam naturally goes with the flow.

His parents may attend to the squeaky wheels in their lives—hectic job, sick grandparent, Cam's difficult sister, or a neighbor in need. They have come to expect that Cam is fine and doing well. Some days, they give Cam just a quick passing smile. He doesn't complain. But if he is passed over too often he may gradually come to feel alone in a busy world. When he sees how worried his parents are, he may not bother them with his problems. In this way, he may take better care of his family than he does of himself. He can become a "little adult." Cam is at risk of losing himself in the lives of others.

Keys to Living with the
Highly Adaptable Child

o **Check in with this child regularly.** Ask, "How are you doing? How are you feeling? Is there anything you want or need? What do you think about . . ." If you, the parent, are intense or high in energy, sit down, slow down, and take slow, deep breaths while you *wait* for your child's answers. Give him time to express himself.

Keys to Living with the Low Energy Child

See also Tarita Turtle, pp. 35–41.

Parent Care

As the parent of a usually cooperative child, your life is different from that of many other parents. Pay attention now so that when you look back in fifteen years you'll be pleased with the choices you made. Heed the still, small voice in your head that knows whether or not Cam is getting what he needs from you now. This flexible child isn't likely to protest if he's getting shortchanged in time and attention. This is the time to build an attentive, strong relationship.

Learning Style

Teachers would love a whole class of Cams. It is effortless for him to please the teacher: he just naturally adapts to most anything she offers that day. Because of his low energy, he spends more time on fine motor skills like art and building with small blocks than on running and jumping. He's easy to keep occupied even on rainy days. Cam readily cooperates with the other children. However, just as he can get overlooked in a busy household, he can easily get overlooked in a bustling classroom. Ask him what he likes most and least. Watch to see that his personal needs are met.

Common Behavior Issues

- **Assertiveness, lack of.** Cam is less assertive than many other children. He doesn't feel a need to be in control because he adapts so naturally. Other toddlers grabbed toys out of Cam's hand. At first, Mom got angry at the other toddlers. Then she coached Cam at home to hold on and say, "My toy." They practiced the "Holding Game" together. In preschool, several more active boys would purposely bump into Cam or his projects. Dad coached Cam to say, in a loud, strong voice, "Leave me alone!" The teacher then came over to help. Soon the boys stopped bothering Cam.

- **Friends.** One of Cam's best friends is quiet and flexible like he is. They get along well together. Cam also has a friend named Tegan Tiger. Cam likes her and doesn't mind that Tegan bosses him around, but Cam's mom doesn't like this behavior. So she arranged for Tegan and Cam to take art classes together. They both liked art, and Tegan wasn't in charge of the class! In kindergarten, Cam sometimes wants to do things *his* way. He practiced using his strong voice with Mom and Dad, so that he could tell Tegan what he wanted.

Words to Help Your Child Live with High Flexibility

Parent

If you lovingly tell your child:

You have needs and wishes, too.

What would you like to do?

Child

Your child learns to say:

I have needs and wishes, too.

I would like to . . .

6

Tarita Turtle
The Low Energy, Easily Discouraged Child

Quiet Tarita Turtle can sit so still inside her shell that one may not notice her at first. Then she proudly stretches her neck and steps out into the world. The moment things don't feel right, she quickly retreats. Tarita retreats when she gets discouraged by toys or other things that are hard to master. When things don't work right away, she pulls back, then quietly goes off to try something else. Because she drops difficult tasks (like getting dressed) and moves on to easier ones (like playing with her toys) she can appear forgetful and disobedient. She needs help more often than other children who are more persistent and less easily frustrated. Therefore, she appears clingy and fragile.

Her natural motto is, "Life is hard." Her parents must work to teach her a more useful motto: "What is an easier way to do this?" In today's busy and complex world, it's good that someone is looking for easier ways to do things! Because Tarita prefers company in case the going gets hard, she is a natural "people person."

Keys to Living with the Low Energy Child

○ **Be realistic.** Tarita has less energy than others her age. Plan activities accordingly. Encourage walking and other moderate exercise where she is not competing with high energy children. She is unlikely to excel at soccer! Help her build fine motor, creative, and intellectual skills.

Keys to Living with the Child Who Is Easily Frustrated

Left to herself, Tarita walks away from play, learning, and daily activities when success isn't immediately obvious. Tarita needs help to learn how to learn.

- **Avoid activities that are too far above her current level of skill.** Observe your child's listening, attention, memory, large and small muscle skills. Some challenge is important, but too much is discouraging. If activities are too difficult, wait a few months and try again.

- **Look for interests, abilities and talents.** Interest creates motivation, and abilities bring success. Build on *your* child's interests and natural talents.

- **Measure out frustration.** Tarita stops when she is too frustrated, so serve up frustration in small, manageable pieces. Limit the *number of frustrating things you fit into a day.* Allow her some choice in how much frustration she takes on: "Do you want me to pour the milk or do you want to?" Do frustrating tasks when she is at her best, probably in the morning. Be sure she gets a good night's sleep.

- **Break tasks into small, easy parts.** Tell her, "First put your foot through the big hole of your pants, then put your foot through the little hole." "To do this puzzle let's look for all the edges (or the pieces with red)." When she reaches age 4, ask, "How can we break this job into parts?" This is an important lifelong thinking skill.

- **Share tasks.** When Tarita reaches 3 or 4, make agreements about what she will do and what you will do: "We need to pick up all the blocks. Do you want to pick up red ones or blue ones?" "Kitty needs food and water. Which one will you give her?"

- **Teach her to ask for *specific* help.** Encourage her to say what she *can* do and then ask for the exact help she needs: "I can cut this with my scissors if you hold the paper for me." Or, "I can cut paper with my scissors, but not this cardboard." She will feel more capable and others will be more willing to help.

- **Offer frequent encouragement.** *Praise effort, not just results:* "I see you're really working hard at that," or, "Good! You're going to go back to try again." Praise partial success: "Look! We've put all the *big* books on the shelf."

Parent Care

- **Expect Tarita to complain!** Tarita Turtle is often discouraged. Life feels harder for her than for other children. She whines more even with the best of parenting. (You're lucky. If she had lots of energy, she would scream instead of whine.) Demonstrate strong and whiny voices. Encourage her to use a strong voice and to ask for help when she needs it.

o *Wants* help or *needs* help? Watch to see what is really needed. Does she need help right now, or want you nearby in case she will need help? (Let her know you are available if needed.) Give help when it is needed, and encouragement when not. What part can she do, and what part does she need help with?

o Plan easy activities, especially late in the day. See page 70.

Learning Style

o Child care/Preschool. In Tarita's first preschool, there were many active children. Tarita couldn't move out of their way fast enough. Sometimes they accidentally ran into her. Tarita felt frightened and miserable. She didn't know how to tell Mommy about it, so she just cried and cried. Mom decided that Tarita needed a more comfortable environment. She found a small home daycare with just five other children. There was plenty of room for the two lively children. Tarita especially liked playing with one quiet friend. She also liked going from place to place to play with whatever she wanted.

o Individual pace. Tarita learns best when effort brings immediate success. Otherwise, learning is frustrating rather than fun. She seldom practices for the sheer joy of mastery. When toys, games, projects, or activities of daily living are difficult, she moves on to something easier. If she wants to learn a specific skill, it's important that she work at her own pace. She needs to feel successful at the first step before moving on to the second. No one learns well when anxious. Frustration makes Tarita anxious—especially when she's alone. She learns best when a helpful parent, teacher, or friend is nearby to help if needed. Alone with frustration, Tarita gives up.

o Small muscle skills. Because Tarita is low in energy, she is more attracted to small muscle skills like drawing, than to big muscle skills like running and jumping. Because she often sits and learns with her eyes, she may suddenly start some new skill that she has learned from watching others, like stringing beads.

Common Behavior Issues

- **Attention seeking.** Before Mom learned about temperament, she expected Tarita to play by herself. But playing is discouraging! Blocks tumble down. Puzzle pieces don't fit. Crayons break. Tarita wanted someone nearby, to help. Over time, she discovered it was easier to throw a block— and get Mom's attention!—than to make a stack of blocks.

    Around 18 months Tarita discovered an easy way to get Dad's attention. (Remember, Tarita is always looking for an easy way!) She grinned and pushed the remote control buttons *again*. Dad tried to be patient, but Tarita pushed the buttons faster and harder. Eventually, Dad realized Tarita's goal was not to play with the remote, but to get attention. Trying to please Tarita by being patient didn't help. So instead, Dad firmly said, "Tarita, you can't be in the family room if you touch the remote. You must go to your room if you touch the remote." He stood at her door for two minutes and wouldn't let her out. He carried her to her room three or four times daily for a week until Tarita learned. (Other children may learn after more or fewer repetitions.)

    Gradually, Mom and Dad accepted the fact that Tarita couldn't play by herself as long as other children. They took turns playing with her. They also arranged play dates with other families, so sometimes they watched several children and sometimes they had time off.

- **Dawdling.** Left by herself, Tarita doesn't get much done. There are two reasons. First, she doesn't have as much natural energy as other children for hopping around and picking up toys. Second, when any task looks difficult she quickly gets discouraged.

    When Tarita went to get dressed, she got stuck getting her shirt or shoes on. Then she'd drift into playing with toys. When Mom told her to go clean her room, she *wanted* to cooperate. But when she got there, there were *too many* toys. She felt so discouraged that she looked at books instead. When Mom came in, she'd demand, "Tarita, why haven't you picked up these toys? Don't you remember what you came in here for?" Mom got upset because she always had to remind Tarita. She didn't like being a nag. When Mom got angry, Tarita felt even more discouraged.

    The same thing happened with brushing her teeth or setting the table. Everyone thought those jobs were easy but they were hard for Tarita. When she whined, "It's too hard," Mom answered, "No, it isn't. Just go do it!" So instead, Tarita began to say, "I didn't hear you," or, "I haven't had time yet," or, "I forgot." Mom would get angry and answer, "Tarita, why don't you ever listen?!"

Once Mom and Dad learned about temperament, they planned things differently. They understood that Tarita wasn't trying to be difficult. Until she's really comfortable, she *needs* someone nearby. She's more relaxed and more *able* to work when she has company. So Tarita brought her clothes to Mom's room, and they got dressed *together*. After a *lot* of practice, getting dressed became easy and Tarita started dressing in her own room. Sometimes she needed to change clothes in the late afternoon when she was tired. It worked better to dress with Mom nearby. Dad no longer expected Tarita to do chores by herself. Instead, they worked as a team. On Saturdays, the cleanup team works in Tarita's room early in the morning, before she gets tired. They start with, "It's time to do this together." Then they cut big jobs into little parts: first, they pick up toys in one corner, or first the animals. They make up silly songs so the work is more fun.

○ **Dependence.** Because Tarita gets frustrated so easily, it takes her a long time to get comfortable doing things all by herself. Without being aware of it, Tarita gradually learned, "If I work slowly enough, Mom or Dad will do things for me." Waiting for Mom became her main way of handling frustration. A better solution is teamwork and breaking things into small parts.

○ **Eating.** Over-eating: Because Tarita gets frustrated easily, she fussed and complained more than other babies and toddlers. The easiest way to soothe her was to give her something to drink or eat. This worked well until the doctor said Tarita was gaining weight too fast. It took more time to figure out and deal with Tarita's frustrations. However, thanks to her parent's effort, her weight returned to normal.

○ **Loss.** When Tarita's Uncle Tad died, Tarita was sad and discouraged. She wanted to see Uncle Tad, just as she always had. The more discouraged she became, the more she seemed to forget how to do the things she had been able to do just a week before. For a while, she depended more than usual on Mom and Dad for help. With time, she became more independent again.

○ **Shyness.** Because Tarita is low in energy, she doesn't jump into active games with the other children. She looks for friends who will help her when she needs it and not make fun of her. She makes good friends. It just takes her a while to find them.

○ **Stubbornness.** Tarita's Aunt Trina complained that Tarita was stubborn. She didn't know that for children like Tarita, stubbornness is made, not born. She expected Tarita to do many things she wasn't able to do, especially by herself. She expected her to dress herself, to hold her spoon the right way, and to practice longer at new games. Everything at Aunt Trina's house was too hard! If Tarita said, "I can't do that," Aunt Trina answered, "Yes, you can! Just try. Don't be a quitter!" Tarita felt discouraged. She accidentally discovered if she said, "I won't do it," Aunt Trina acted differently. She stood silently and glared at Tarita. Sometimes she called Mom to come early to get Tarita. Tarita and Aunt Trina never got along well. Sadly, Aunt Trina never understood why.

○ **Weaning.** Tarita weaned later than active youngsters who prefer to be on the move with bottle or cup in hand. Tarita wasn't in a hurry to go anywhere! She liked to cuddle with Mom. Mom waited until Tarita could drink easily from a cup. She cut the morning nursing first because that's when Tarita handles frustration more easily.

Words to Help Your Child Live
with Frustration while Learning

Parent
If you lovingly tell your child:

Everyone gets frustrated. It's what you do next that counts.

You like to work on a team. (Or, Tell me if you need help)

This will get easier with practice. Everyone has to practice.

How can we break this into small parts?

What part can you do? And what part do you need help with?

Let's take a short break and come back.

You'll know when you're ready to do this by yourself.

You've learned other things. You can learn this, too.

Child
Your child learns to say:

Everyone gets frustrated. It's what I do next that counts.

I like to work on a team. (Or, I'll tell you if I need help.)

This will get easier with practice. Everyone has to practice.

How can I break this into small parts?

What part can I do? And what part do I need help with?

I'll take a short break and come back.

I'll know when I'm ready to do this by myself.

I've learned other things. I can learn this, too.

Tarita shares these behavior issues with other children in this book. For more help, see:

- Child care/Preschool, pp. 71–72.
- Potty training, pp. 109–112.
- Self-esteem, low, pp. 78–80.
- Separation, pp. 81–82.
- Sibling rivalry, pp. 112–114.
- Sleep, pp. 102–109.
- Temper tantrums, pp. 91–94.
- Testing rules, page 97.

7

Fenson Fawn
The Sensitive, Intense, Cautious Child

Fenson Fawn is naturally sensitive and cautious. Only when conditions are exactly right does he stand up and step into the clearing in the woods. No amount of coaxing or yelling brings him out sooner. When he feels cautious, he feels very, very cautious. Because he is intense, *all* his feelings are strong.

Fenson practices new things in his mind long before he practices with his body. Although it takes him longer to get started, with time he becomes as comfortable and confident as other children. Fenson becomes anxious if pushed into situations before he is ready. The fight or flight hormone, adrenaline, pours into his blood stream. His heart pounds and his hands get sweaty. He feels truly afraid. His body freezes up, just like any other fawn that hides by lying perfectly still. It isn't so much that he will not move, but that he *cannot* move.

In new situations, Fenson *looks* before he leaps. He *enjoys* watching and learns a great deal that way. He stands on the sidelines at his best friend's birthday party. Afterwards, he tells his parents all about it with as much pleasure as if he had played the games and tasted all the treats.

Keys to Living with the Sensitive Child

o **Help Fenson *feel* comfortable.** Remember walking with a rock in your shoe? Fenson likely feels the same about the seam in his sock or tag in his shirt. Cut out the tags and choose comfortable clothes. A comfortable body calms the mind. Over time, help him take care of his own sensitive body.

Keys to Living with the Intense Child

See also Tegan Tiger, pp. 49–58.

Keys to Living with the Cautious Child

o **Expect caution in all that is new.** Dad gives him time to watch and practice in his head before joining in. At the park, they watch other children on the slide. "Would you like to slide?" asks Dad. "No!" answers Fenson. So Dad takes him each day to *watch* the other children. While Dad waits, he tells himself, "In time, Fenson will be ready."

Grandpa gets frustrated and tries to push Fenson into new situations before he is ready. But Mom says, "If we push him too fast, he will become more and more afraid of new situations. People don't like to feel *really* frightened. For Fenson, it's better to move slowly into new situations. When he goes at his own pace, his body can relax. Then he gradually learns to feel more comfortable when facing new things."

o **Divide new tasks into small steps.** Fenson practices new things step by step. For several weeks, he climbed up and down the stairs of the slide, without once sliding down. This is how his internal sense of security grows. With each practiced step, he learns what comes next. The more life feels familiar, the more secure he feels.

o **Provide relaxed companionship in new situations.** When Fenson is ready, Dad holds him as they slide down the slide. Fenson holds on for dear life! After several weeks, Fenson wants to try all by himself. If his parents were to always take his first "No!" as the final answer, Fenson's life would be very narrow. As he grows older, Fenson learns to take on new things with a teacher or a friend for company.

Parent Care

In a society which glorifies assertiveness and independence, you're likely to get some critical glances. Those who don't understand temperament will believe your over-protectiveness created Fenson's caution. Know in your heart that this sensitive being arrived on your doorstep with his own inborn temperament. You are creating a safe, comfortable environment in which he can grow and flourish.

Learning Style

o **Child care/Preschool.** Like other cautious children, Fenson does best in a program with structure and consistency. Then there aren't too many new things at once. His teacher tells the children ahead of time what is going to happen. Having older children around gives Fenson a chance to watch new things before he tries them.

When Fenson started at his new child care center, Dad stayed with him much longer than the other parents stayed with their children. For many days Fenson sat on the side and watched. It looked like he wasn't doing anything at all. But in his mind, he was practicing the activities and the school routine. Neither Dad nor his teachers pushed him. They invited him, but let him go at his own pace. When he was ready, he joined in.

Mom has learned that when Fenson gets all the sleep he needs and snacks when he is hungry, he has more emotional energy to cope with new things that come along each day. She keeps afternoons and evenings as routine as possible. Late in the day, Fenson is less able to handle new activities or experiences.

Fenson learns mainly with his eyes. Teachers call him a *visual* learner. At preschool, he watched every day for a week as a classmate put a puzzle together. The next week, Fenson easily put it together by himself.

Common Behavior Issues

○ **Activities and lessons.** Before signing up for lessons (such as swimming, art, or music), Mom takes Fenson to watch several sessions. Then, when he is ready, Mom pays so he can join in.

○ **Danger.** Mom knew Fenson would need time to get comfortable at the new swimming pool. As usual in new situations, Fenson hung back in fear, watching others splash and swim. Mom talked with him about what they saw. After he'd become comfortable, Mom remembered the safety rules for the pool: "Don't run near the pool. Never go in the pool alone." Fenson objected to the rules. Mom calmly told him the rules again on several occasions. She reminded herself that Fenson was objecting to the newness of the rules, not necessarily the rules themselves.

○ **Eating.** Fenson likes to stick to familiar foods. When he was a baby, he wrinkled his nose and pushed out all new foods. Dad then learned to dab a bit of the same new food on Fenson's lips several times a day for several days. Often, by the eighth or twelfth taste, Fenson realized he liked apricots or applesauce. However, he never liked new foods when he was really hungry or tired. As a toddler, he would eat mashed carrots, but scream at carrot pieces in soup. They seemed too different! His sensitive body has to take in so many new things that he wanted his food to always be just the same from one time to the next.

As a preschooler, Fenson still eats only a few foods. Mom loves all kinds of interesting, different foods. But she knows Fenson has his own way with food, and it's important not to get in fights about what he eats. She knows that combining milk or cheese or beans with wheat or rice gives Fenson as much protein as meat. Because he eats so few fruits or vegetables, she also gives him a daily vitamin so that he gets the nutrition he needs. At age 5, he still doesn't eat nearly as many different foods as his adventuresome cousin. But sometimes at a party or picnic, he'll try a new food after watching other children eat it.

○ Friends, choice of. Boys like Fenson may have high or low energy. If low, it will likely affect his choice of friends. Beginning around 4 years, Fenson saw that he could not keep up with the high energy boys in preschool. As a result, he prefers to play with the girls, who are calmer. At first, this bothered his mom. Then she said, "Fenson isn't going to be a soccer star, but he'll be someone's sensitive partner."

○ New events. Many ordinary, but new events frighten Fenson Fawn. Even a phone call from Grandma can frighten him. At first, when she called, he just listened on the phone. Grandma said, "Hello, Fenson! How are you?" To help, Dad started asking Fenson beforehand, "What do you want to tell Grandma today?" Then Fenson could practice, "Hi, Grandma. I go watch swimming lessons with Mommy." Finally he was ready for the real thing, and Grandma was delighted.

Before the family traveled to visit Uncle Paul in Tennessee, they looked at books about airplanes. They talked about exactly what would happen: check-in counter, security line, meals, and bath-room. Then they played "travel." They packed his suitcase and lined up chairs like airplane seats. For a week, Fenson slept in the sleeping bag he would take. They practiced saying, "Hello, Uncle Paul." Mom told him where they would sleep, and what they might see. They looked at pictures of Uncle Paul and his family. Mom called Uncle Paul to remind him that Fenson might need some space at first. Fenson would likely be ready for hugs and kisses after he'd had a day to warm up. All the preparation took time and effort. However, it was worth it. The whole family enjoyed the trip. Because many things were familiar, Fenson relaxed and had fun.

- **Separation.** Fenson is less upset about Mom going out than about having a new sitter. So Mom asks a new sitter to come by a couple times just to get acquainted. When he was little, Mom first left him for only 15 or 20 minutes at a time. Once he was used to the sitter, she left him for longer periods. When possible, Mom found sitters who could come to their house, rather than taking Fenson to the sitter's house. That way, Fenson didn't have to get used to a new sitter *and* a new house.

- **Stress.** Given his strong feelings and the time he needs to get used to new things, it's not surprising that Fenson is upset by life's big changes. His emotional stress often shows up in regression. When under stress, he's often unable to do things he could do before. After moving to a new house, Fenson kept having potty accidents, so his parents put him back in diapers for six weeks. For a month after starting in a new child care center, Fenson seemed unable to feed himself or get dressed by himself. For three weeks after Grandpa died, he couldn't remember his job of setting the table. Family illness, divorce, and other such stresses usually bring a similar reaction to children of this temperament.

  As he got older, Fenson asked *lots* of questions about things that worried him. He asked some questions again and again, even though his parents gave good, clear answers. His parents felt frustrated, but they realized he needed time and repetition to make sense of new things. He needed to update the pictures in his mind about how life works. "Why did Grandpa die? Is heaven in the ground where they put him?" Dad listened patiently and talked with Fenson about his feelings and his worries. Dad said, "People die when they get very old. Mom and I are not old so we will be here to take care of you. I miss Grandpa a lot. I feel sad. Do you feel sad, too?"

  Mom knew Fenson would have to work with this big, new issue for a long time. She found some books at the library about death, which Fenson wanted to read again and again. Each afternoon when they came home, they buried a leaf or flower in the garden. They talked about the new plants that would grow. Some days Mom was tired and rushed. She had little patience to stop to bury *another* leaf. But she could see that repeating this ritual again and again helped Fenson gradually accept the mystery of life.

- **Testing limits.** Because he doesn't like new things, Fenson needs time to get used to new rules and routines. As much as possible, his parents tell him about new rules ahead of time: "We are getting a new living room carpet tomorrow. After that, we can only eat at the table." Fenson always complains that new rules aren't fair, but Mom just repeats them calmly. After the new carpet arrived, he needed more calm, clear reminding. He wasn't trying to be disobedient. It just takes Fenson time to adjust. For a week, Mom consistently reminded him: "Fenson, we don't want spills on the new carpet. Where do we eat now?" When Fenson complained and wouldn't go to the table, Dad calmly picked up his plate and took it to the table. Unfortunately, some grape juice spilled on the carpet. Thinking back, Mom realized it would have been better to change the eating rule *a week before* the new carpet arrived.

Words to Help Your Child Live with High Sensitivity

Parent
If you lovingly tell your child:

You notice things that other people don't.

Many people aren't bothered by people, noise, and bright lights all around them. You're learning to take a break when you need one, so you can feel calm again.

How can we make your body feel better?

You are good at noticing how other people feel.

Child
Your child learns to say:

I notice things that other people don't.

Other people aren't bothered by people, noise and bright lights all around them. I'm learning to take a break when I need one, so I can feel calm again.

How can I make my body feel better?

I am good at noticing how other people feel.

Words to Help Your Child Live with High Intensity

See also Tegan Tiger, page 57.

Words to Help Your Child Live with Caution

Parent	Child
If you lovingly tell your child:	**Your child learns to say:**
You don't like surprises.	*I don't like surprises.*
You like to know what's coming.	*I like to know what's coming.*
You need time to get used to new things.	*I need time to get used to new things.*
You can practice in your mind to get ready.	*I can practice in my mind to get ready.*
You know when you are ready.	*I know when I am ready.*
Tell me when you are ready.	*I'll tell you when I am ready.*

Fenson shares these behavior issues with other children in this book. For more help, see:

- Biting and hitting, pp. 90–91.
- Potty training, pp. 109–112.
- Sleep, pp. 102–109.

8

Tegan Tiger
The Intense,
Slow to Adapt Child

There are no minor events in the life of Tegan Tiger. All her feelings are big. She is either rolling in delight or roaring in anger. As a small child, her intensity rose faster than her words could come out, so she bit and hit instead.

Tegan is intense *and* slow to adapt. Transitions and changes are hard. The higher her intensity, the harder it is to change course. She becomes a high-powered engine caught on a circular track. Even transitions she's made hundreds of times before are hard—waking up, setting aside a toy before lunch, getting into the car. People who don't understand temperament call her bossy and stubborn, but refusing to go with the flow is her way of saying, "Wait! I can't change that fast!" Under her roar is a natural planner—a soul that feels more secure when she knows what's coming and there are few surprises.

Keys to Living with the Intense Child

o **Tantrums are routine during Tegan's early years.** Fortunately, yelling and tantrums are not life-threatening—even though they sound like it! If parents often back off for fear of Tegan's strong reactions, then Tegan's intensity rules the household. (And Tegan will be frightened by how much people resent her.) Tegan's moment-to-moment happiness is less important than the needs and well-being of the whole family. Her intense reactions will blow over sooner if parents stay calm and firm.

o **Expect things to get worse before they get better.** When you change a rule or routine or enforce a limit, Tegan will not accept with grace. There will be protest until the new normal is established. Parents imagine running a peaceful household, but Tegan cannot keep the peace. Her yells of protest do not measure how well you are doing as a parent.

- **Avoid the intensity spiral.** Intensity fuels intensity. When Mom yells, "Stop that!" or, "Be quiet!" Tegan's intensity rises. Instead, Mom tries to lower her own intensity. She takes several deep breaths and talks in a soft, quiet voice. She keeps her hands at her sides. Mom pretends she is a calm newspaper reporter: "Tegan, I can see you are really disappointed and angry that we have to leave early today," or, "Use your words. Don't hit." Later by herself, Mom may yell into her pillow or jog to let off steam. As much as possible, however, she acts calm when Tegan is intense. Dad tells himself, "This is just intensity. I can stay quiet and firm."

- **Channel intensity into forms you can live with.** Singing and drama are great outlets for intense emotions. Make up stories and plays with stuffed animals.

- **Teeter-totter effect.** Tegan lives on an emotional teeter-totter. When her intensity is high, her adaptability is low. Flexibility increases only as intensity comes down. Even happy occasions, like birthday parties, raise emotional intensity. Then adaptability drops. The key is learning to bring intensity down *before* it skyrockets. Look carefully for the early signs.

Keys to Living with a Natural Planner

See also Walla Whale, pp. 54–67.

Parent Care

- **Discount sale.** Tegan seems to exaggerate everything, but that's how big her feelings really are. Tegan's mom finally understood that Tegan gets upset by *every little* thing. Intense children learn that intensity alone can bring adults running. Mom learned to think like she does at a "30% off" sale. The real price, or the real problem, is 30 percent less than it sounds at first. Thinking this way helps Mom stay calm. If it's not a real emergency, Mom no longer runs.

- **Parent preference.** It is normal that Tegan, when young, always demands one particular parent when she's uncomfortable. (Think of babies out on the plains in ancient times—better they not take time to consider which parent to go to when a wild animal steps into view.) Unfortunately, the other parent can then feel left out. This tendency is often strong at 2 and fades by 4. In the meantime, Dad spends time with Tegan when Mom is not around because then he quickly becomes her favorite person of the time. At 2 years, Mom and Dad wanted to take turns with the bedtime routine, but Tegan screamed for Mom. Instead, Dad started doing baths *every* night, and Mom read books *every* night. Once Tegan got used to the new routine, things went much better.

o **Lack of respect?** Grandpa complained, "When you tell Tegan to do something, she should do it right away!" Mom explained, "Tegan isn't trying to be bad or disrespectful. She can't make fast changes. Many of us live in a 4-wheel drive vehicle that can go anywhere. Tegan lives in a train on a track—she has to build a new track before she can go somewhere different." Grandpa still didn't get it. Mom thought, "Maybe Grandpa is also slow to adapt."

Learning Style

o **Child care/Preschool.** Mom carefully picked a preschool for Tegan. She looked for balance between planned and unplanned time. Mom knew that a regular schedule was easier for Tegan to picture in her head. On the other hand, Tegan needs more time than other children to shift from one activity to another. She needs teachers who understand and help her with transitions. Free floating games with other children use up a lot of adaptation energy. When she was little, Tegan could only handle short periods of give-and-take with other children. She gets along best in small groups her own age, with those who are not especially active. Large groups get too intense. Younger children are unpredictable. Older children and very active ones overwhelm her—she can't adapt quickly enough to keep up.

At 4½, Tegan's behavior at home suddenly became much worse. She started misbehaving more, hitting her brother, and having tantrums about everything. Her parents were discouraged. Things were much worse than just a few months before. Mom also thought it was just a phase. Dad thought they needed firmer discipline. Tegan's teacher reported that Tegan was terrific and seemed well adjusted. Her parents wondered what they were doing wrong.

They made an appointment with a child psychologist. Mom went to observe at Tegan's new school. She noticed how loud the room was. Tegan wandered from activity to activity without really becoming involved. When she finally started a project, she needed to stop because it was time for a group activity. The psychologist suggested they try a different school—quieter, with fewer children, and where the activities were more structured, but would allow Tegan to move at her own pace. Tegan's behavior at home improved immediately and remarkably. Tegan had been unable to say how stressed she had felt. She had used all her adaptation energy at school and had none left when she got home. Her newest school was calm and predictable. She felt secure while playing and learning. Even though the old school was excellent, it hadn't been a good fit for Tegan.

When Tegan started kindergarten, she made plans with Dad. At the beginning she sometimes went to the school library instead of out to recess. There, she could more easily stay calm, and there was less to adapt to than on a playground full of children. At lunch time, she sat at the edge of the playground to eat. There was too much going on out in the middle! One by one, Mom invited two of her classmates home for playdates so Tegan could get to know them. Finally, Tegan had friends to play with at recess.

Common Behavior Issues

- **Afternoons are awful.** At the end of the day, Tegan was often upset and grouchy. By the time she got home from school, she'd used up her whole tank of adaptation energy. Mom gradually learned to plan very routine afternoons and evenings. Life became easier for everyone.

- **Arguing.** When Tegan turned 4, Aunt Sarah moved to town. Once Tegan got to know her, she liked to visit overnight. Every time Aunt Sarah asked Tegan to do something, like brush her teeth, Tegan argued. She'd say, "I can't brush my teeth now because I might want a snack," or, "Teddy Bear hasn't brushed his teeth yet," or, "You're not the boss of me." Aunt Sarah found Tegan difficult. Mom explained: "Because Tegan is slow to adapt, she argues while she gets ready to make a change." Aunt Sarah changed her approach. She'd say, "Tegan, let's play 'Candyland' after dinner. We'll set the timer for 20 minutes. Then it will be time to brush your teeth and read one story. If you don't brush your teeth by 8:30 p.m., we won't have time to read a story." When Tegan could see the whole plan in her mind ahead of time, she didn't argue nearly so much.

- **Breath holding.** One day when Tegan was 18 months old, Mom walked into the living room and found Tegan scribbling on the wall with crayons. Mom took the crayons away. Tegan got upset because she liked making the wall pretty. She stamped her feet and grabbed Mom's hand but Mom wouldn't give her the crayons. Tegan got so angry and her body got so tight that she didn't breathe. Her face turned from angry red to grayish blue. Mom got very frightened! She called Tegan's name and patted her, but nothing helped. Finally, Tegan started to breathe again. Mom was so relieved she burst into tears. Mom called the doctor. Because he knew Tegan was in good physical health, he said, "This can happen with very intense children. Even if she held her breath so long that she passed out, she would automatically start breathing again. It looks frightening, but isn't dangerous." The same thing happened several more times. Once Tegan learned to talk and yell angry words, she no longer held her breath.

○ **Cries when greeted by parents.** Tegan often cries when Mom picks her up at child care. She cries because it's another transition, her adaptation energy has been drained, and her feelings are strong.

○ **Safety.** Tegan adapts slowly to new rules—including safety rules. The more strongly (or intensely) the rule is stated, the harder it is for Tegan to change course and follow the rule. One day Tegan was so excited going to a birthday party that she forgot to wait at the corner for Mom. Another day her ball rolled into the street. Tegan's attention was on the *ball*. Dad shouted, "Tegan! Stop!" When Tegan heard his intense voice, she became more tense and anxious, but her higher intensity was still focused on the ball. She ran faster into the street. Luckily, there were no cars coming. Dad was really scared! When Tegan is intense, she is *less able* to shift her thinking. Her parents now pay special attention when Tegan's intensity is high, or they are near dangerous places. (See "Impulsiveness," pp. 75–77.)

○ **Divorce, coping with.** Cousin Tyla is also an intense natural planner. After much difficulty at home, her parents divorced. They hoped Tyla would adjust quickly, but changes are hard for Tyla. It was hard to live in two different houses. It was especially hard because schedules and family rules were very different in each house. Tyla's stubbornness and tantrums showed how unhappy she was. Her parents met with a therapist, who said, "Tyla can't manage so many changes. To help Tyla, *you* need to make changes so schedules and rules are more similar in both houses." Fortunately, her parents were able to set their own feelings aside to make compromises for Tyla. As life became more similar in both houses, Tyla felt more secure and happier.

- **Doctor's visits.** Tegan practices the steps ahead of time on a doll, so visits will be familiar. Mom found a doctor who moves slowly and says what's going to happen next.

- **Eating.** As an intense baby, Tegan was either full or starving. Sometimes she wasn't hungry when the clock said it was mealtime. If Mom got worried and pushed a spoon of food in her mouth, Tegan vomited. She wasn't sick; she was upset because Mom was upset and her stomach got too tight to hold food. Tegan doesn't waste her limited adaptation energy on something as basic as eating. At 10 months, she demanded the same blue cup and the same few foods.

  At 2 years, she always wanted her food the same way—toast cut into triangles, potatoes mashed, not in soup. Being slow to adapt, she doesn't like her personal space being suddenly crowded. That made it hard to get used to a bib and a high chair. Tegan wakes slowly and she's not hungry until she is fully awake about 9 a.m. Mom found child care where Tegan could eat breakfast when she got hungry. Over the years, she never felt hungry when she was excited or sad or angry.

  Cousin Tyla, who is slow to adapt and intense like Tegan, is *also* very sensitive. With these three traits, she is a very picky eater. As a baby, Tyla screamed if there were too many lumps in her mashed bananas. At 2, she wouldn't eat a different brand of chicken soup because the flavor was different. At 4, Mom and Tyla put a seven-day breakfast menu on the refrigerator. Mornings were much easier when Tyla knew ahead of time what would be for breakfast.

- **Head banging.** At 14 months, Tegan pulled the cat's tail. Mom said, "You can pat kitty or stroke kitty like this. Don't pull kitty's tail." Tegan pulled kitty's tail again. Mom repeated the rule and added, "I'm putting kitty outside so her tail won't get hurt." Tegan was very frustrated. She really wanted to play with the kitty. She got so angry she hit her head on the floor. Mom was horrified. She'd never seen such a thing.

  Several weeks later, Mom took Tegan's shirt off for a bath. Tegan wanted her shirt on. She was so frustrated! She put her own wrist in her mouth and bit so hard she left teeth marks. Again, Mom was scared. She called a temperament counselor, who said, "Many intense, natural planners react this way. Fortunately, this phase will pass as Tegan learns to talk instead." When Tegan hit her head on the carpet, Mom talked to her in a soothing voice. One day Tegan banged her head on the cement walkway. Mom carried her inside, kicking and screaming, to her bed, where she wouldn't hurt herself.

○ **Hurt feelings.** Tegan's cousin, Tyla, is an intense natural planner who is also very sensitive. At age 4, a friend teased Tyla. Being sensitive, Tyla's feelings were hurt. Mom walked over to hug Tyla, but Tyla pushed her and yelled, "Go away! Leave me alone!" Tyla crawled under the table, shouting, "I hate you. I hate my life!" Mom was surprised and confused. She didn't know this is a common reaction for children like Tyla. Because Tyla is slow to adapt, she doesn't like people crowding into her space— even to give comfort. The more intense her feelings, the more she hates being crowded. A while later, she climbed out, and said, "I want to go to the park." Over time, Tyla has learned that she needs time by herself to calm down. Fortunately, Mom stayed calm when Tyla shouted at her. Later, they talked about the problem with her friend and about what she could do differently next time.

○ **Moodiness.** Tegan gets moody because her feelings are so big. She's never just pleased or disappointed. She's *delighted* or *devastated.* Her friend BayLee gets moody because there are so many frustrating bumps in his path. In the early years, bad moods often become tantrums especially when the child is tired or hungry. At 4, Tegan had major mood swings. Fours are all-or-nothing thinkers, so at any given moment Tegan sees herself as either fantastic or a complete failure. When she's 7 or 8, she'll be able to understand that she is a good person who sometimes makes mistakes. At 4, she lives on a roller coaster. Tegan's parents used to be upset by her moodiness. Now they tell themselves, "She's training for the theater."

○ **Perfectionism.** Tegan always wants things "just so." Even at 4, she had a picture in her mind of what she wanted to draw. If her drawing looked different from the picture in her mind, she cried and tore it up. (Tegan has a fast-adapting friend, Cam. When his drawing doesn't match the picture in his head, he can quickly change the picture in his head.) Tegan enjoys art more when she can trace a picture or color in a coloring book. Dad showed her pictures of abstract art that were about colors and feelings rather than about drawing a house or a person. That was more fun for Tegan.

○ **Separation.** Between 18 and 24 months, Tegan had difficulty with separation. She missed Mom, but mainly, she didn't like the changes and transitions. Mom arranged several short visits to a new sitter or child care. Once Tegan had new mind pictures, she was fine. To make separation easier, Mom always sang the same song to the tune of "The Farmer in the Dell": "To Isabel's house we go. To Isabel's house we go. . . . .You'll eat lunch and have a nap and then I'll pick you up."

When Tegan was little, she always took her favorite pillow to child care. Now she takes a favorite toy. At 3, Tegan liked to push Mom out the child care door. That helped her feel in control of the separation. When the sitter comes to their house, Mom tells her all Tegan's routines. When Tegan is sick, or tired, or when there is family stress, she is more upset by separation.

○ **Stomach aches, diarrhea, and vomiting.** Cousin Tyla is an intense, natural planner and also quite sensitive. Every time Tyla started a new class or child care, she complained of stomach aches. Mom thought Tyla was pretending or making excuses. She called the doctor. The doctor said, "She is not pretending. Tyla's body reacts to the stress of new things. She may get stomach aches or diarrhea." Mom slowed things down. She took Tyla for short visits first. In June, Mom took her to visit her September preschool. Mom also arranged to visit with a girl one year older, who had just finished that class. The older girl told Tyla about the new teacher, the classroom rules, and what to expect. Tyla built pictures in her head of what to expect and her body felt better in September.

One day at 14 months, Tegan was tired and frustrated. She'd just had three tantrums. Mom decided to put Tegan in her crib until she fell asleep. Tegan screamed until her whole body was tight. Her stomach was so tight she vomited. A month later, Tegan vomited when she didn't want to be in her car seat and on other occasions as well. Gradually, Tegan unconsciously learned that she could *make* her stomach so tight that she vomited. One day, Dad really needed to leave a party early. Tegan didn't want to go and started to scream. Then Tegan tightened her stomach and vomited! Dad had to stay longer to clean up. Dad called the temperament counselor, who said, "Vomiting usually happens when families get caught in intensity spirals." As Tegan's parents learned to work with their own intensity, and with Tegan's, the vomiting stopped.

○ **Stubbornness.** Tegan always has a picture in her mind of what she expects to happen next. It takes time to change those pictures. When Mom suddenly tells her to stop what she's doing, Tegan's natural reaction is, "No!" Stopping right now doesn't fit the picture in her head. If Mom gets angry and punishes, Tegan gets more intense and less able to adapt. She gets even more stubborn. Fortunately, Mom has learned that mental pictures have to change before behavior can change. When others complain that Tegan is strong willed and stubborn, Mom answers, "Tegan has a mind of her own. It will be useful when she grows up."

○ **Weaning.** For Tegan, the picture of comfort is Mom's breast. Comfort and food—what could be better! Not surprisingly, Tegan weaned later than other children. Mom introduced a bottle, and later a cup, right after breakfast. Tegan is more adaptable early in the day and when she's not too hungry.

Once Tegan was comfortable with bottle and cup, Mom stopped nursing even though Tegan complained. Tegan continued a bottle to smooth the morning transition from sleeping to waking. And it helped calm her tense body before bedtime. Friends said Tegan should give up the bottle by age 2. But Mom said, "Two will be one of the hardest years of her life. She'll need all the help she can get." But the dentist was worried about Tegan's teeth, so Dad gradually diluted the milk—one half ounce less milk and one half ounce more water every few days. Soon it was all water, so tooth decay was no longer an issue. Dad said to himself, "I'm sure she won't take the bottle to high school."

Words to Help Your Child Live with High Intensity

See also, "Describe feelings," page 94.

Parent	Child
If you lovingly tell your child:	**Your child learns to say:**
You have big, strong feelings.	*I have big strong feelings.*
Your feelings are big and strong and like a fire truck (or race horse).	*My feelings are big and strong and like a fire truck (or race horse).*
How big or fast are your feelings right now?	*How big or fast are my feelings right now?*
What can help your fire truck (or race horse) settle down?	*What can help my fire truck (or race horse) settle down?*
You're learning to control your fire truck (or race horse.)	*I'm learning to control my fire truck (or race horse).*
You can think and plan better when your fire truck (or race horse) is resting.	*I can think and plan better when my fire truck (or race horse) is resting.*

Words to Help Your Child Live
as a Natural Planner

See also Walla Whale, page 67.

Tegan Tiger shares these behaviors issues with other children in this book. For more help, see:

- Biting and hitting, pp. 90–91.
- Discipline, pp. 96–102.
- Potty training, pp. 109–112.
- Sibling rivalry, pp. 112–114.
- Sleep, pp. 102–109.
- Temper tantrums, pp. 91–94.
- Testing limits, pp. 46–47.

⑨

Walla Whale
The Active,
Slow to Adapt Child

Walla is moved by huge, natural forces. Strong tides and great waves keep her constantly in motion. Even though she is sleek and beautiful, she cannot turn on a dime. There is something solid and unchanging about Walla Whale. She is both constantly in motion and in charge of her own course. Because she needs time to change course, she naturally plans ahead. *She is a natural planner.* Sea captains respect her energy and power. Wise captains don't expect her to respond instantly, as a television does to a channel changer. Instead, successful captains plan ahead before setting sail with such a great creature.

Walla Whale is high in energy and slow to adapt. Her energy pushes her out into lots of life experiences. Those same experiences bring new, unexpected rules. This internal struggle creates waves of feelings that are hard to manage.

Keys to Living with a
Natural Planner

○ **Adaptation energy.** Cars have different-sized gas tanks. Similarly, people are born with larger or smaller tanks of "adaptation energy." Walla Whale has a very small tank of mental energy for making changes. She instinctively rations the little adaptation energy she has, so she demands her favorite doll each night and her familiar blue cup at breakfast. (Dad got several identical blue cups to make his life easier.) Routines save adaptation energy.

Just as the car's gas tank runs low toward the end of a trip, adaptation energy runs low toward the end of the day. The lower the sun is in the sky, the harder it is for Walla to shift from her expectations. Even an unexpected detour on the way home from child care can cause a tantrum. Her parents try to keep afternoons and evenings as routine as possible. Sleep refills adaptation energy. For the day to go smoothly, Walla needs a full night's sleep beforehand.

○ **Mind pictures.** Instead of calling Walla "slow to adapt," Mom calls her a "natural planner." Even at age 2, she lives with a running video in her mind of what she expects to happen next. If she pictures wearing her red skirt, the purple one will not do. If she pictures a trip to Meadow Park, then Brookside Park is wrong! Before she can change her behavior, she needs time to change the picture in her mind. Her parents' job is, as much as possible, to tell her what is ahead, so she can make *accurate* pictures in her mind.

○ **Plan ahead.** The more Walla knows about what is ahead, the more easily she can make transitions and changes. At age 1, Mom made up words to the tune of "Twinkle, Twinkle Little Star" to let Walla know that a diaper change was coming. At 2, Dad pointed out the routines that make life more predictable: after lunch it will be nap time; we put on pajamas and *then* look at books. At 2½, an egg timer marked time to get out of the bathtub.

Around 2½ Walla had a really hard time. Mom would ask, "Do you want milk or water with lunch?" Walla would choose one and then scream for the other. At this age, she had no sense of time. If she said "No" to milk it felt like she would *never* have milk again. Mom made her choices easier: "Do you want your glass empty or with milk?" Sometimes she simply didn't offer choices.

At 3, Dad put a one-week calendar in Walla's room. He put seven papers on her wall, with stick figures or pictures to show what *usually* happens each day—days the family is together, days in child care, who will do pick-up and drop-off, etc. Each night, they look at the next day, and discuss what may be different, such as a doctor's appointment or shopping trip. Each morning, they review the plan. At 4, Mom announces trips to the library or bedtime five or 15 minutes beforehand. A timer from www.timetimer.com helps Walla easily *see* how time is passing.

At 4, Walla can understand time and more complicated ideas. Mom and Dad tell her about Plan A and Plan B. "If it rains tomorrow we will . . . If it's sunny, we will . . ." This makes life easier for everyone. Because Walla can see both plans in her mind ahead of time, she can easily step into either one when the time comes.

○ **Rules and rituals.** Walla *loves* routines (once they are familiar). She feels more secure when she knows what will happen next. She thrives on knowing:

Her sandwich is always cut in triangles, not squares.
Duck Duck goes in the bathtub before she gets in.
She slides down the slide twice before leaving the park.
Mom gives her two kisses at bedtime.

At 4, the rituals are more complex and life is easier. Walla looks out at the thermometer to see if she needs a coat. They have a weekly breakfast menu with French toast every Tuesday.

○ **Transitions.** Shifting from one familiar activity to another is a transition—playing to eating, indoors to outdoors, waking to sleeping. Changes include a broken toy, a shopping trip, illness, vacation, a new family rule, a parent away on business, a move, or new baby. Those who are fast adapting slip though these transitions and changes like a relaxed swimmer who glides through the river of life. With low adaptability, one has to pause, plan, and jump from each rock to the next. This is especially hard during the early years when so much of life is unfamiliar.

When possible, Walla's parents make only a few changes at a time. Life goes more smoothly when Walla has time to get comfortable with one thing before adjusting to another. The more she knows about the future, the more secure and relaxed she feels.

Parent Care

See also BayLee Bluebird, pp. 68–69.

Take a deep look at yourself. Often the difficult job of parenting Walla is made challenging because of parent agendas—needing her to move quickly or swim to a place she's not yet ready to go. Pushing a whale is hard work. Slow down; learn her agenda; plan ahead. Understand her needs and direction. Learn how to row with her flow. When Walla does "blow," don't take it personally. Use these meltdowns as opportunities to learn and make a better plan for next time. As her parent, you are the waterway director. You monitor the rise and fall of the tides, set clear guidelines and limits, and follow through on your commitments. Work with this great whale power by looking, whenever possible, for win-win solutions—ways you can both get what you need.

Learning Style

Walla learns more by doing than by watching because of her high energy. A whale wouldn't stop swimming and lie on the beach. To keep herself still takes all her attention, so there is no attention left over for learning. That's why she learns more easily when she can move. Direct Walla's energy, rather than try to stop it.

- **Child care/Preschool.** Because she requires time to adapt, Walla needs extra time to settle into a new child care or school situation. Daddy takes her to visit ahead of time and stays with her so she can get used to where things are and how things work. Once she's on her own, she settles in in three stages. First, she holds back to study even more carefully what goes on. As a natural planner, she's filing pictures in her mind about how this new school works. Second, with her high energy, she tests all the rules, to see if they will change. Third, when the new pictures are clear, and she knows the rules are firm and friendly, she feels comfortable and can focus on friends and play.

  Humans have survived over the ages by constantly hunting for food and chasing children. It's not surprising that many aren't designed for sitting still. Because of all her energy, Walla learns better when she can walk, rock, wiggle, or doodle while she learns. The teacher seats Walla *behind* a sensitive classmate who is otherwise bothered by Walla's movements. (A sensitive teacher would be a more difficult problem.)

  Group size. With 25 toddlers or preschoolers around, no one can tell for sure what is going to happen next. Because Walla likes to know what's coming next, Mom looked for a small home child care. She couldn't find one that suited their schedule but she did find a smaller preschool with fifteen children. Even there, Walla had trouble making new friends. Mom wanted to arrange some one-to-one playdates with a classmate to help Walla make new friends. She asked the teacher who would likely be a good playmate for Walla.

Common Behavior Issues

- **Attention, not paying enough.** High energy Walla is always on the go, living her busy life. She takes in information primarily with her *body*, not her ears. Don't bother talking to her back. To get her attention, touch her shoulder and make eye contact.

- **Cuddle, refuses.** It's hard to cuddle with a whale that is always on the move. Aunt Jenny's feelings were hurt because Walla wouldn't snuggle with her. Mom said, "She likes *you*, she just doesn't like being still." Mom advised, "Don't take care of her by holding her. Instead, take care of her by going places with her. Help her by telling her ahead of time what is going to happen next. That will be easier for both of you!"

- **Divorce/Loss.** Walla's dependent side doesn't often show. High energy makes her look independent and ready to run her own life. When her parents divorced, they thought she would handle the change just fine, but her stress came out indirectly, away from home. Walla liked kindergarten, and because it had been going well before the divorce, she put even more energy into learning new games at recess, helping the teacher pass out projects, and serving snacks.

  On the other hand, she started fighting more with her two best friends. Any time friends disagreed with her, Walla was afraid they would leave as Daddy had. Mom and her teacher told her that people can have different ideas and still get along. They reassured her, "Your friend isn't going to leave."

  Mom knew that children with Walla's temperament often don't talk a lot about their feelings. The kindergarten teacher asked Walla to make sad pictures and angry pictures. Sometimes Walla covered many pages with dark blue and purple scribbles. Mom read library books about divorce and told her often, "Daddy went away because he was upset with Mommy, not upset with you."

  Not surprisingly, Walla was more moody. It seemed that her tank of adaptation energy had shrunk. She got more upset than usual whenever plans and routines changed. Mom tried to keep as many things the same as possible. Once Daddy got settled in his new apartment, Walla could visit him on weekends.

- **Eating.** Walla hated having a bib tied around her neck. It made her feel like the world was closing in on her. At her auntie's house, she never wore a bib. Auntie just changed her shirts more often than Mom did.

  Eating out. After a whole day of adapting, Walla is in no shape for dinner out in a restaurant. After many tantrums and leaving restaurants without finishing, they decided to go out for brunch instead. At first, they only went to restaurants with a play area. As Walla grew older, they went to a cafe that had booths so there was more room to wiggle. Only as she reached school age, did they go to restaurants where Walla needed to sit in a chair.

Same foods. For weeks at a time, Walla ate the same foods day after day. When she thought about food, she saw pictures in her head of bananas and yogurt. Mom kept only good, nutritious food in the house.

At preschool, and sometimes at a party, Walla tried new foods and even used a napkin. When she got home, however, she insisted on her same old favorites. Mom felt annoyed until she realized, "Walla uses up her adaptation energy at school. When she comes home, she has very little adaptation energy left." Because there were always so many new and changing things in life, Walla felt more secure when at least her food stayed the same, day in and day out, weekdays and weekends. Mom gave Walla a daily vitamin to assure the nutrition she needed.

One day, during spring break, Mom put three peas on Walla's lunch plate. Mom choose lunch rather than dinner, when Walla was less tired. Peas didn't look like food to Walla; she didn't eat them. For the next five days, Mom put three peas on her plate. Mom said "Yum!" and ate them before she took Walla's plate away. On the sixth day, Walla tried one. After several more days, she began to like them.

Self-feeding. At 6 months, Walla wanted to feed herself. Dad put a plastic sheet under her high chair. Finger foods were easy for Mom to serve. She thickened yogurt with baby cereal, so Walla could scoop it up with her fingers. Grandma felt differently. She liked feeding with a spoon because it gave her a special connection with her grandchildren. But Walla repeatedly pushed Grandma's spoon away. She cried and banged on the tray for finger foods. Finally they found a compromise. Grandma gave her finger foods and a spoon to hold. Every once in a while, Grandma slipped a spoonful of pureed apricots into Walla's mouth. Grandma felt happy to be part of Walla's life in this way.

Skips breakfast. For Walla, waking up is a big transition that takes time. She's not hungry until about 10 a.m. Mom packs a bag of cereal for her to eat in the car. She also found a small home child care in which Walla could eat when she was hungry.

o **Friends.** Because Walla is on the move, she runs to any children who are playing nearby even though fitting in doesn't come easily for her. All toddlers are self-centered, but children with Walla's temperament appear especially self-centered. When another child reached out to share her toy, she screamed and sometimes bit. Mom then held Walla on her lap for a brief time-out. Walla was always anxious to get off her mom's lap and play. As she learned to use words, she hit and bit less often.

Being the boss. When Walla runs the show, she doesn't have to spend so much adaptation energy adjusting to others. So she wants friends to play her way. She prefers to make the rules and tell others what and how to play. She likes playing with more adaptable children who are willing to let her be the boss. Of course, if they are younger, it's even easier for her to be the boss.

On the other hand, like BayLee Bluebird, Walla is attracted by the physical skill of older children. Being with older children is good for Walla. She learns that when she screams and hits, they won't let her play. And they won't let her be the boss all the time. Consequently, she *has* to practice cooperation.

Because Walla naturally wants to be a leader, she needed time to learn the give-and-take of friendship. Her parents helped her learn. At age 5, Mom told Walla, "Tarita doesn't want to come play because she never gets to choose the games or make the rules." Mom suggested, "Maybe Tarita will play with you if you use the timer and take turns being the leader." Mom added, "Sometimes, a good leader finds out where others want to go and then leads them there. What games does Tarita like to play? Because you like to plan ahead, you might ask Tarita, 'What do you want to play after we finish this game?'" Mom then asked, "What else do you think might help?"

During the learning process, there were some sparks and friction. However, getting the help she needed, Walla learned to be a better friend by the end of kindergarten.

Time of day. Baby Walla did much better in a morning play group when she still had more adaptation energy. Similarly, at age 4, unstructured play with friends worked fine in the morning. But in the afternoon, it was better to have a plan ahead of time, so Walla had less to adapt to.

Wanting to win. Walla likes rules because then she knows what to expect. She likes to make sure that other children follow the rules. Walla also likes to win. Sometimes, when she is afraid of losing, she says, "I didn't hear that rule," or, "*That* rule is wrong!" Sometimes the teacher suggests they play games where there are no winners or losers. Uncle Jed knows that it's hard to lose a game when you're young. When Walla and Uncle Jed play games, he asks,

"Do you want to play game rules or Walla rules?" When Walla makes the rules, she *always* wins. Some days, she is able to play the game rules.

○ **Lying.** When Walla was 4, Mom took her Christmas shopping. Walla ran down an aisle and bumped an ornament off the shelf. She felt very upset that something bad had suddenly happened. She told her mother, "Santa Claus flew by and broke it!" Mom knew Walla couldn't make sudden changes, so she picked up the ornament and paid for it. That night she said, "I know it was an accident that the ornament broke. Sometimes accidents happen. Next time, please tell me the truth—that it was an accident." Mom knew that helping Walla make a positive plan would work better than telling her *not* to lie.

○ **Talks too much or too loudly.** Because Walla has so much energy, her voice is loud, like the roar of the ocean. Learning to talk more quietly is a slow process, something that some children can't master until age 4. Mom and Walla practice taking turns with loud, outdoor voices and quiet, indoor voices. Mom praises Walla when she remembers her quiet voice.

Walla hates to hear Mom say, "Don't talk so loud!" When Walla needs a reminder, Mom silently puts a finger to her lips or begins to whisper. Because Walla has to listen carefully, it helps her remember. When Walla yells at Dad, he says calmly, "I can't hear you when you yell," and waits for her to talk more quietly.

With so much energy, Walla has a lot to say. Sometimes Mom says, "I can't listen right now. I'm listening to the words in my own head," or "I can't listen now because I have to pay attention to the cars." Walla may continue talking, but at least she knows that Mom won't be listening.

Dinners were difficult because everyone talked at once. Mom found a picture of a mouth and three pictures of ears. They took turns passing the pictures around. When Walla had a picture of an ear in front of her, it helped her remember to listen.

○ **Trips are terrible.** After a visit to their grandparents during the winter and to Disneyland during the summer, Mom never wanted to go on another trip with Walla! Walla had so much energy that she charged out into new places. By the second day, she had run out of adaptation energy. The third day was one meltdown after another. Mom and Dad decided to plan differently: they kept afternoons easy and bedtime regular. After two days at Disneyland, they went to a beach or park for the rest of the vacation so there weren't new rules every day. They told Walla about plans and rules ahead of time. The next trip went much better.

Words to Help Your Child Live as a Natural Planner

Parent	Child
If you lovingly tell your child:	**Your child learns to say:**
You need time to change the picture in your head.	*I need time to change the picture in my head.*
You like little things to stay the same so you have energy to make important changes.	*I like little things to stay the same so I have energy to make important changes.*
You like to do things at the same time and in the same way because then you feel more peaceful.	*I like to do things at the same time and in the same way because then I feel more peaceful.*
In a few days (weeks), you'll be comfortable with this new situation.	*In a few days (weeks), I'll be comfortable with this new situation.*

Words to Help Your Child Live with High Energy

See also BayLee Bluebird, page 84.

Walla Whale shares these behaviors with other children profiled in this book. For more help, see:

- Discipline, pp. 96–102.
- Eating, page 74.
- Impulsiveness, pp. 75–77.
- Potty training, pp. 109–112.
- Safety, page 93.
- Sleep, pp. 102–109.
- Weaning, page 83.

10

BayLee Bluebird
The Active,
Easily Frustrated Child

BayLee Bluebird is always on the move and in a hurry to get somewhere. He goes places and does things—spreads his wings and flies. He tries to fly over gates or rules that block his way. He gets frustrated by things that are hard to learn; he drops them and looks for something that is easier to do. Because he gets discouraged when things are hard, he depends on adults for help. He flits between independence and dependence: two flaps forward and one flap back.

Keys to Living with an Active Child

o **Exercise.** BayLee needs to work off a bundle of physical energy every single morning, afternoon, and often evening as well. Like a purebred Dalmatian (Dalmatians were bred to run beside coaches for 30 miles a day), he'll tear up the house if he doesn't get enough exercise. How long does it take your child to actually get physically tired? Match exercise with current physical skills. Many activities below will use more energy if shared with another child.

Chores. Children can vacuum, carry groceries, scrub floors with a brush, carry clothes to and from the laundry, help make beds, rake the yard, water with a watering can.

Classes. Look for action rather than waiting in line. Which will fit your child better: Team sports like soccer, or individual sports like swimming? Competition or not?

Indoors. Turn the child's bed into a trampoline: put away the bed frame and put the mattress on the floor. Build a slide with sofa pillows. Provide a rocking horse, riding toy, mini-trampoline, skates, hippity-hop ball. Fill old socks with rice, tie them closed and throw them into the laundry basket. Hang a punching pillow in a doorway. Put books or canned goods in the laundry basket to push around the house. Race, jump, or hop up and down the hall, or put chairs at opposite ends of the room to run around. Pull other kids around on a blanket.

Who said the bathtub is only for bathing? Isometric exercises use muscle tension without movement: "Push hard here and hold up the wall while I count to 10 or sing a song." Dance to music, exercise and dance videos. Have a rug or corner of one room as the area where wrestling, pillow fights, and play tug-of-war can happen.

Once they slow down, try Play-Doh®, cars and trucks, finger paint in the bathtub, cardboard box from a washing machine for a playhouse, big crayons and paper, etc.

Outdoors. For toddlers and 2s, generally use a harness instead of a stroller for outings. Walk or run around the block, visit parks, hike. Get out in the rain and snow as long as the weather is not dangerous. (Buy warm clothes so *you* are also comfortable being outdoors.) Use riding toys, trikes, bikes, scooters and skates, balls to chase. Visit shopping malls and gyms and high school tracks. Dad parked several blocks from child care so BayLee got a good run before child care and back to the car at the end of the day. Once BayLee was old enough, and because the neighborhood was safe, Dad dropped BayLee off a block from home so he could run the final stretch.

Keys to Living with a Child
Who Is Frustrated by Limits

Rather than accept the frustration of limits, BayLee uses his energy to push past them. He goes back again and again and again to things he's told not to do—climb on the bathroom counter, run out the front door, and chase the cat.

O Buzz. BayLee's mind often got locked into things. One day when BayLee was 4, Dad got an idea while they were reading. When BayLee reached to turn the page, Dad held it down and said, "The page is stuck. We can only look at this page." Dad pointed to things on the same page. BayLee tried again to turn the page, but Dad repeated, "It's stuck." Then Dad said, "Buzz is the magic word. If we say Buzz, the page will turn." It did! They played this game for a week. Then Dad said, "Sometimes your mind gets stuck on one idea, like the book gets stuck on one page. When your mind gets stuck, let's say Buzz so you can think of something else." Later that day, BayLee's mind got stuck on climbing the back fence after Dad had told him not to. Dad said, "BayLee, I wonder if your mind is stuck." They both said, "BUZZ." With practice, Buzz helped Bay Lee get unstuck and think of other things to do.

○ **Choose your battles.** Mom put a lock at the top of the front door so BayLee couldn't reach it even when he pulled a chair over. Because the cat always moved faster than BayLee, Mom left that issue to the cat. Mom focused on removing BayLee from the bathroom counter.

○ **Hold the line.** Pushing past one limit gives BayLee the hope of pushing past another. Mom had to be more persistent than BayLee. She took him down from the counter repeatedly, and put him in his room for two minutes each time. After about 20 times, BayLee stopped.

Keys to Living with a Child Who Is Discouraged or Frustrated by Learning

See also Tarita Turtle, pp. 35–41.

BayLee's energy pushes him up and out, then frustration pulls him down and back. Independence then dependence is a continual dance of two steps forward, one step back. Don't compare his milestones (weaning, potty training, etc.) with those of other children. He's on his own schedule.

Parent Care

○ **Create a village.** BayLee's energy can cause *parent burnout*. Get needed relief from other family members, play groups, friends, and child care. Invite or hire an older child to come play at your house. BayLee's mom feels she is the master of ceremonies at a three-ring circus. When he was little, his parents took turns so each could sleep. Later, they set up a babysitting exchange with other families.

○ **Plan easy activities, especially late in the day.** As the day wears on, easily frustrated BayLee and Tarita get emotionally worn out. After a day of child care, they are less able to manage frustration, so they act up more and are less able to entertain themselves when they get home. Evenings go better if Mom spends a few minutes snuggling with Tarita, rather than rushing right off to fix dinner. Afterwards, Tarita plays nearby with easy things, like her small plastic animals or big crayons and paper.

Active BayLee is used to rocking on a rocking horse by the kitchen door while Mom fixes dinner. At 3 years, Dad put a picture list on the refrigerator to remind him of things he likes to do. At 4, Dad puts on a dance or exercise video for BayLee while he fixes dinner.

○ **Walk, don't run.** To easily frustrated children (especially if they are also intense), frustration feels like an emergency. Don't feed this false belief by *rushing* to their side.

Learning Style

Active toddlers have more energy than skill, so they run and jump and climb. BayLee learns mainly by *doing,* rather than watching. He learns to get dressed by dressing; to pour milk by pouring. He learns colors as he scribbles with crayons. In school, he most easily learns the letters by tracing his finger over their shapes or running around the big letters painted on the playground. Because he learns with his body, teachers say he is a *kinesthetic* learner.

○ **Child care/Preschool.** BayLee's first preschool was a disaster. He couldn't sit still in the long circle time, he wouldn't print letters as the other children did, or lie on his mat during rest time. He cried and hit. Mom had to find a new school.

She looked for a school with active, older children and an energetic teacher who could match BayLee's pace. With his high energy, BayLee crawled, walked, and jumped sooner than others his age. Now he likes to play with older children who match his energy and skill. He also *behaves* better with older children. If he doesn't follow their rules, they won't let him play. This school had plenty of outdoor space, and children could play outdoors as much as they wanted. Mornings started with a walk in the neighborhood or dancing. In the afternoon, they had "track time," to circle the yard on bikes and scooters.

These teachers knew that high-energy children often learn fine motor skills later than low-energy children. They offered painting and drawing instead of printing so BayLee could feel more successful as he practiced fine motor movements. (Note that it's not until age 7 than many normal children can accurately remember the correct order of the strokes in each letter. The more children practice incorrectly, the harder it will be to read their writing over time. Earlier is not always better.) Mom knew she had found the right school when she saw another child with BayLee's temperament who was happy and well liked by the teachers.

○ **Frustration.** Everyone learns better when calm, rather than anxious. Frustration makes BayLee feel anxious. Even feeling afraid of *becoming frustrated* makes him anxious. It helps to learn in steps. First, he learned to put big Duplo® blocks together, then smaller Lego® blocks. He learned to fasten big buttons before trying small ones.

BayLee is also a people person. He learns more easily when there is a trusted parent, teacher, or friend to give help when he needs it. Like everyone else, BayLee learns better when his mind is fresh. That's usually in the morning.

○ **Separation and adjustment.** BayLee missed Mommy and Daddy during child care. He worked extra hard to take care of himself during the day. By the time he got home, he'd had as much frustration as he could handle in a day. Having been away, he also wondered if Mommy and Daddy still loved him. He needed much more help than usual. He wanted Daddy to feed him dinner. After a few weeks, BayLee learned that his teacher was a good helper, too. He began to like school and didn't miss Mommy and Daddy so much. Gradually, he was again able to do more for himself at home.

For more about learning, see "The Bear Cubs," pp. 86–89.

Common Behavior Issues

○ **Anger.** BayLee is often upset with his parents. He's frustrated by the limits they set and hates waiting for the help he needs. Mom knows BayLee's mood is better when he's had enough sleep and isn't hungry. She also knows he needs more support at the end of the day. Mom works to provide enjoyable activities that are more fun than frustrating late in the day.

○ **Attention seeking.** See Tarita Turtle, page 38.

○ **Bad words.** Many children try "bad words" when they turn 4. BayLee was hoping for the excitement of seeing Dad upset. Because Dad ignored the words, it wasn't any fun. Branson's mom said very calmly, "We don't use that word in our house" or "I don't understand that word." When Tegan called her mother stupid, Mom named the feeling under Tegan's upset: "I see you are really disappointed."

- **Blaming others.** All small children blame their parents when things go wrong. BayLee blames more than usual. He gives up easily and stops trying; when he doesn't get what he wants, he feels helpless. He doesn't feel in control of his surroundings. He believes other people have more control. When something goes wrong, it must be their fault—parents, teachers, or friends. The more he learns to work with his own temperament, the less he needs to blame others.

- **Boredom.** BayLee can't stick with things as well as other children. As soon as something gets hard he moves on to something else. He gets frustrated by drawing and complicated Lego® projects. Rather than say, "I can't do this," he often says (with words or actions), "I'm bored."

- **Dependence and demands for help.** BayLee needs help with more things for longer periods of time than other children do. He comes to a standstill with problems that others hardly notice, like pulling on his pants. This is especially true when he's tired after a whole day of dealing with other frustrations. Sometimes food and rest can restore his independent side. Mom plans difficult activities, like a doctor's appointment, in the mornings. BayLee is at his best then. Mom plans easy activities in the afternoon.

  As Dad learned more about temperament, he found that working as a team is better than nagging. BayLee feels much more secure when someone else is around to lend a hand in case the going gets tough. Instead of trying to push BayLee into independence before he was ready, Mom and Dad decided to stick by him until he was ready to be on his own. For example, when dressing, BayLee did one side while Mom did the other. From time to time, Mom said, "You'll know when you are ready to do this by yourself." One day, many months later, BayLee was ready to get dressed by himself. Dad and BayLee set the table together. Dad tells him, "You're a people person. You like working with other people."

  BayLee's friend has a temperament much like BayLee's, except Branson's body rhythms are also very irregular. He gets tired and hungry at different times of day. When he is awake and well fed, he is very independent. When he is either tired or hungry, his dependent, clingy side shows more than usual. His mom has more difficulty than BayLee's mom in predicting how any particular day will go.

○ **Eating.** A bluebird is always on the move. BayLee burns energy quickly and gets hungry often. Mom keeps easy, healthy snacks on a shelf where BayLee can stand and eat: crackers, cubes of cheese, orange sections, or defrosted frozen peas. BayLee can fly in and snack like a jet plane that refuels in midflight. However, for safety, Mom taught him to stop and eat, rather than run with food in his mouth. Mom didn't want crumbs all over the house, either. Whenever BayLee left the kitchen with food, Mom brought him back to the kitchen, saying, "Food stays in the kitchen." BayLee screamed. Finally, he learned that he could only eat in the kitchen. Usually he eats half his dinner while dancing around the kitchen as Mom cooks. He's able to sit for only a few minutes at the family dinner table. As he grew, he became able to sit for longer periods.

Sometimes, when he's really tired, he doesn't eat any dinner at all. And sometimes he gets so frustrated and anxious wanting the dessert that he can't eat his dinner. Mom decided he could eat his tiny dessert at the end or the beginning of dinner. She knew it wouldn't fill him up, and there were no second helpings of dessert.

This on-the-go and backwards meal plan has been hard for Dad. He wasn't raised this way. Mom, however, is very active and remembers how she hated sitting at the table when she was little. A meal plan that suits BayLee's temperament means less stress for everyone. After BayLee had settled into kindergarten, they started having one special family dinner each week. They lit candles and everyone sat at the table together. By then, BayLee had so much to say about school that he was able to sit at the table for 10 or 15 minutes.

○ **Friendly with strangers.** Because BayLee is active and likes to talk, he meets people easily. He's also learned that many different adults can help when he gets stuck—Mommy and Daddy, Auntie and Uncle, Grandma and Grandpa, baby sitters, and teachers. One day, Mom was late picking BayLee up after school and she found him by himself, talking with a total stranger. At first, Mom was frightened. She hadn't thought that BayLee might rely on any adult for help. Mom decided to talk with BayLee about safety and strangers. She told him people to ask for help from were teachers, policemen, or store clerks. He should never get in a stranger's car, because Mom would not know where he was, and Mom would worry. Though Mom had been frightened that day, she knew BayLee's trait would be helpful in adulthood. "BayLee automatically connects with other people to get things done. He will be a terrific networker!"

○ **Friends, trouble with.** Because BayLee is so active, he can run, skip, and hop much better than others his age. He prefers to be around older children to practice and learn more physical skills. If he lived in a small village, he would naturally play with active, older children.

Getting along with friends is not always easy. Early on, he had trouble sharing toys. Waiting for his turn was hard! He got frustrated when the rules of a game got in his way. Other children sometimes called him a "baby" or a "cheater." They didn't want him on their team. Gradually, he found out that if he wanted to play with the older children he had to follow the rules. Playing with older children was a good way to learn.

When BayLee turned 3, Dad talked about being part of a team. "On a team you need to wait your turn." They talked about how hard it is to wait. They thought of things to do while waiting. For example, in kick ball, he could practice kicking imaginary balls while he waited his turn. Or he could imagine sliding down the slide until his turn came. Dad and BayLee keep talking about how team players act. Dad encourages him and knows that with time he'll be able to be a better sport.

○ **Help, begging for help then refusing.** There is a constant battle going on inside BayLee: the active, independent side fights with his easily discouraged side. He cries, "Mommy, Mommy, I can't reach the toothpaste!" When Mommy reaches for the toothpaste, BayLee screams, "No! I want to do it myself!" It's always tempting to step in and do things for BayLee. Sometimes it's better to wait and watch. At 4, BayLee was able to think and solve problems. Things went more smoothly when Mom asked, "I wonder what might work?" or "How did you solve this before?" or "What part do you need help with?"

○ **Impulsiveness.** BayLee has a friend, Comeback Bear Cub, who is both curious and very active. He crashes into safety limits more often than others. When his muscles demand exercise, he moves. He climbed up the living room bookcases, scooted up the stepladder that Dad left out, slipped into the park's goldfish pond, and hopped inside the frozen food display at the grocery store. He loves exploring.

He isn't trying to drive his parents crazy, but he does need more time, attention, and support than other children. No wonder Mom and Dad decided they needed a safety plan. First, they made a list with three parts:

Life-threatening or serious injury
> Falling on top of the floor furnace
> Running in the street or parking lot
> Falling into Rapid River

Injury, pain, possible broken bones, but not life-threatening
> Falling off the kitchen counter
> Falling off the stepladder
> Touching the oven door with fingertips

Nuisance for Mom and Dad
> Falling in the backyard mud
> Pouring out the cat litter
> Making messes with food and drink

They then covered the floor furnace with a solid wooden frame and decided not to visit Rapid River for a long time. That left cars: "Always hold on to my hand in the street. In the grocery parking lot, hold hands, or hold the grocery cart." Mom felt calmer when she realized fewer things were really dangerous.

Comeback Bear Cub repeatedly tests the rules. His parents use a strong, stern voice if he runs too close to the street without holding hands. They try to use a calmer voice at other times, so Comeback learns that streets are more dangerous than pouring out the kitty litter. When Comeback was little, they usually used a safety harness. And Mom always took his hand, saying, "We hold hands in the street."

It's easier for Comeback to listen before his intensity rises. So his parents talk about rules ahead of time. Dad reminds Comeback by asking, "How will you stay safe in the parking lot?" (If Comeback forgets to hold Dad's hand, Dad takes him back to the car. Of course, Comeback screamed while Dad held his hand against the car for a moment.) When possible, they also talk about *new* rules ahead of time: "We're about to cross the bridge. The rail is for looking through." When Comeback started to climb the rail, Dad took him down and repeated the rule.

It also helped to practice safety rules. They made up a game called "parking lot." They set up chairs to be the car, and practiced the rule: "In the parking lot, hold Dad's hand, or touch the car." Sometimes Dad pretended to be the child so Comeback could be the dad. Before bedtime stories, they review one safety rule. "Why do we hold hands in the street?" Thinking about a rule when he is calm helps Comeback see the rule more clearly in his mind.

Comeback's parents pondered why mellow Cam Chameleon had self-control at age 2, while Comeback still had little at age 4. Dad saw that Comeback had much more energy, curiosity, and intensity. "It's like Cam drives a little Volkswagen with Volkswagen brakes. And that works just fine. Comeback is in a giant semi-truck, so the same little brakes don't work. It takes longer for his brakes [the front part of his brain] to grow strong enough to match his big engine."

Dad then wondered, "Is self-control more like a muscle that gets stronger with practice? Or is it more like a water bottle—the more you use it the faster it's empty?" Mom replied, "On any given day, it's like a water bottle. The more Comeback needs to use it, the sooner it's empty. That's why he is so difficult after a day at school. But in the long run, self-control is like a muscle. If he didn't have to use it at all, it wouldn't grow stronger." "Well," answered Dad, "that means we have to look for the balance between teaching more self-control and not demanding too much."

They looked for small ways to practice impulse control. They played "start-stop." Comeback told Mom to start talking, walking, or jumping and then said, "Stop." Then they traded places. They played red-light, green-light. They held hands and said a short gratitude prayer before eating dinner. They broke long jobs into short jobs: "Let's pick up the books and do ten jumping jacks," then "Let's pick up the blocks and do ten deep knee bends." While waiting in lines, they said to each other, "I can wait! I can wait," or "Patience pays,"or they counted. Saying the words out loud helped Comeback learn to say them inside his head.

o **Lying.** "Have you brushed your teeth, BayLee?" "Did you put your socks in the laundry?" "Did you do your chores?" By age 4, BayLee usually knew the answers Mom and Dad wanted to hear. He didn't want to upset them, so he said, "Yes!" Mom got angry because BayLee's answers weren't true. Dad said, "In the United States, we have a Fifth Amendment. Adults don't have to admit they are guilty. So why do we expect BayLee to?" Instead, Dad started saying, "BayLee, let's go brush our teeth," or, "Your socks are still on the floor. Let's go pick them up," or as he got older, "Come do your homework near me, so you can tell me if you need help." BayLee felt much better.

o **Pleasure seeking.** BayLee is naturally drawn to things that are fun. He sticks with things as long as they are more fun than frustrating. He's much less interested in finishing a project than in having fun along the way. In our busy, workaholic world, we need people to remind us to live in the present and have fun along the way.

o **Running off.** BayLee's friend, Comeback Bear Cub, is active and very curious. He is drawn like a magnet to everything new and different. He's a world-class explorer. His mom needs a full-time nanny on roller skates! Whenever they go out, Comeback bolts off to check out interesting sights. Mom has learned to limit trips to fascinating places like stores. Early on, she used a harness when they went for walks. (Active Comeback hated sitting in a stroller.) As he got older, Mom used the harness only as a consequence of running too far ahead or into the street.

At 3 they played the stop-start game. They took turns telling each other, "Stop!" and "Go!" They practiced stopping talking, singing, clapping, walking, and jumping. This was good practice for going on adventures. When Comeback turned 4, it paid off. Mom could use the game when he needed it outdoors.

o **Screen time, demands more.** BayLee loves to watch videos because they offer frustration-free success. Furthermore, video games are carefully designed to find each child's sweet spot between boredom and frustration. There is excitement and success without too much frustration. As such, video games can become addictive for children as young as 4. Set appropriate limits. Choose times when you most need children to be diverted, such as fixing hurried, weeknight dinners. Avoid screen time after dinner, as direct light into the eyes can delay output of the brain's sleep-causing hormone, melatonin. Be aware that you may get a burst of frantic high energy as a rebound effect from screen time—which is why some families ban screen time completely.

o **Self-esteem, low.** When something becomes frustrating, BayLee leaves it and moves on to something else. Moving on gets him out of painful feelings of frustration and discouragement. Around age 4, BayLee began to notice that his friends could do things he couldn't. They could do puzzles and use scissors. Some could draw houses and stick-figure people. He began to think there was something wrong with him. He gradually decided that he must not be as smart as the other children. He felt bad about himself.

Fortunately, BayLee's parents realized that he was having trouble with self-esteem. They knew BayLee was just as smart as the other children, but BayLee didn't practice as much as they did.

Practicing came naturally to other children, but not to him. Because BayLee didn't practice as much, he couldn't do as much. Here are things they did to help.

Describe BayLee's experience. Mom stopped saying, "Oh, that's easy. Just do it!" Instead, she reported what she saw: "That looks hard. That looks really hard!" or, "That looks easy for you to do!" When BayLee looked discouraged or frustrated, she named the feelings so that BayLee could identify them. Dad said, "It's okay to be discouraged. Lots of people get discouraged. What counts is what you do next." Gradually, BayLee had new ways to talk about his life. He and his family could talk about things BayLee needed help with, things that needed practice, and things he had learned to do.

The "Can Do" Chart

Easy	Hard	Want to learn
Can do alone	*Do together*	*Small parts and practice*
Get cap off toothpaste	*Set table*	*Put cap on toothpaste*
Remove seat belt	*Feed the cat*	*Use scissors*
Put on socks	*Put on shirt*	*Use can opener*

When Mom and BayLee looked at the chart, they started with things BayLee could already do, which helped build his confidence.

BayLee told Mom things to write (or draw, or paste a picture of) in each column. They kept looking for ways to divide things into small, easy parts. One day BayLee squeezed the can opener handles while Dad turned the knob. Now that he could do that, they moved the can opener to the "do together" column.

At their weekly family meeting, they talked about the chart. BayLee told Mom when to move something to a new column. BayLee felt proud when he moved things to the "easy" column.

Learn to practice. Dad helped BayLee practice a little bit at a time. He'd say, "Let's set the timer for three minutes and practice using scissors."

As BayLee learned to practice, he learned to do more and more. Slowly, he started feeling better about himself. He learned he was as smart as the other children. Gradually, BayLee learned he didn't have to *avoid* challenges. He just needed to take them in small, steady steps.

BayLee's friend Branson with similar temperament also began to think he wasn't very smart. He became more and more discouraged. In kindergarten, some children could print their names. For Branson, it was hard to make letters. So he decided, "Why even try? I'm not smart like they are." His papers were often blank or messy. His teacher frowned at them and he felt embarrassed. Because he felt embarrassed, he said things like, "Writing is stupid." Unfortunately, no one took time to figure out why Branson was discouraged.

○ **Self-soothing.** How does a flitting bird relax? BayLee sucks his thumb, rubs his belly button, and twists his hair. These are active *and* relaxing. One day, Auntie found BayLee masturbating on the living room floor. She said, "BayLee, the place to do that is in private, in your bedroom. That's where big people do it."

BayLee needed soothing things to do in public that wouldn't bother others or cause teasing. BayLee and Dad made up "secret wiggles." BayLee could:

- Put his feet on the floor and wiggle his toes inside his shoes.
- Run his tongue back and forth just behind his teeth (with mouth closed).
- Put his hands under his thighs, then press first one thigh, then the other, down against a hand.
- Put one hand on his chin with the thumb under the jaw bone, then wiggle the thumb.
- Hold one hand in the other and rub a thumb in the palm of the opposite hand.

There are lots of secret ways to wiggle.

No one thinks well when anxious. Frustration makes BayLee anxious. When BayLee turned 5, Mom asked, "How do you feel inside when things are hard?" BayLee answered, "All tight and wiggly." Mom then suggested, "When you feel tight and wiggly inside, you could take a break or get some help." BayLee decided that when he needed a break, he would skip around the living room three times. (Tarita Turtle, who is less active but also easily frustrated, pets the cat or sings a song when she needs a break.)

o **Separation.** There are two issues related to separation.

Clinging to Mom. Even as an infant, BayLee got frustrated. He didn't just wait for milk, he screamed until it came. He got really annoyed when he couldn't quite sit up yet, couldn't quite crawl, or couldn't quite reach the toy he wanted. His life was out of control; he felt helpless. At such times, he needed someone to take those bad feelings away. Better yet, he needed someone to keep those feelings away. Fortunately for BayLee, Mom learned how to predict and prevent frustration. If she wasn't going to nurse, she warmed a bottle just before he woke up from a nap. She propped him up when he wanted to sit. She watched BayLee and passed the desired toy. Mom could read BayLee's smallest cues. BayLee loved it! He wanted Mom close by, always. Not surprisingly, if Mom wasn't around, BayLee's cry told the whole world he was upset. Between 7 and 9 months, BayLee cried every time Mom stepped into another room. He worried when he didn't know where she was. For a few weeks, Mom sang or talked loudly from the other room so he knew she was close by.

Dad worked long hours. Because he spent much less time with BayLee, he couldn't read him as well as Mom. Mom told him BayLee's private little signals. For example, he lifted his chin when he wanted to be picked up, but there were many other little signals that Dad *couldn't* read. When BayLee was with Dad, he cried and called for Mom. Dad felt hurt and left out. BayLee didn't appreciate how hard Dad tried. Around age 3, things got much better because BayLee could use words to tell Dad what he wanted.

Baby sitters and child care. Mom wisely introduced BayLee to a regular sitter before he reached the separation anxiety stage at 7 months. She started by leaving him for very short periods. The sitter learned to read his cues, so BayLee felt comfortable with either Mom or with her.

As a toddler and preschooler, it was easier for BayLee to go to the sitter's house than have the sitter come to his. He likes new adventures in interesting places. Mom made sure BayLee had a reminder of home. As a baby, BayLee had his favorite blanket. At 2, Mom put a family picture in the back of BayLee's cubby at preschool. Sometimes BayLee took a special toy as well. At age 5, BayLee's lunch box is a good reminder of home.

Starting with a new sitter or child care is hard for BayLee. Would the new caretaker be as helpful as Mommy? At first, he cried every time he got frustrated and Mom wasn't there to help. Mom told the teacher about the things that were hard, like getting a sweater on. The teacher said, "Whenever you need help, BayLee, call me and I'll help you."

Gradually, BayLee learned that his teacher was a good helper. As he trusted her more, he missed Mom less. Special days like field trips could bring unexpected frustrations. Mom and the teacher talked with him ahead of time so that as much as possible, he knew what to expect.

Even though BayLee cries or complains at the time, Mom always tells him ahead of time that she is leaving. She doesn't want BayLee to always be worried about when she might suddenly be gone. Not surprisingly, BayLee misses Mom even more during the evening, when he's already had a day full of frustrations.

At 4, BayLee still hated to see Mom on the phone. Mom didn't like interruptions, and BayLee never knew how long the call would last. How would he get help? So they worked out a plan. After that, Mom asked, "Do you need any help before I call my friend?" or, "What's something easy and fun you can do near me while I'm on the phone?" They also set up hand signals, so when the phone rang, Mom could signal BayLee if the call would be short, long, or unknown. Everyone felt better.

○ **Speech may come later.** Because of his energy, BayLee automatically uses his big muscles for running and jumping. Talking is a small muscle skill. That's why some such children talk a little later than others. BayLee's parents knew that life would be easier once BayLee could communicate. At 6 months they started using sign language. They copied signs that BayLee used, like putting his arms up when he wanted to be picked up. They made up signs for things that were important to him, like patting the side of his high chair twice when he wanted to get down. They also reminded themselves to talk to him slowly and clearly and to repeat important words. Look for more information on "Baby Sign" and check with your doctor if you are unsure about your child's language development.

○ **Stuttering.** For a time, while learning to talk, BayLee stuttered. It was worse when he was tired or excited. His thoughts ran faster than his mouth. He got frustrated because people didn't understand him. The more frustrated he got, the worse the words came out. Because Mom is high in energy, she finished his sentences for him. But the doctor said, "BayLee doesn't need help going faster. He needs help slowing down." So Mom took slow deep breaths to remind herself to slow down. She said more slowly to BayLee, "I have time to listen. What do you want to tell me?"

o **Trouble, attracted to.** Sometimes it seems that BayLee looks for ways to annoy people. He tickles, teases, and interrupts. He repeatedly does things he knows he's not to do. He pulls on electric cords, turns the bathroom faucet on full force, and pours his juice on the table to see its pattern. Mom became a constant nag— "BayLee, don't . . ." Under her breath, Mom called him BayLee the Bug, because he was always bugging people. As Mom learned about temperament, she kept track of when BayLee was most annoying. Usually it was near the end of the day. BayLee was tired from a full day of frustrations. The easy thing to do was to annoy someone, causing an adult to take over and tell him what to do next. When his mom understood this pattern, she looked for ways to make BayLee her assistant, rather than her enemy: "BayLee, I need your help. Can you bring a diaper for the baby? Can you hold the dustpan for me? Can you wash these vegetables? Can you carry these socks to the washing machine? Thank you so much for helping!" When BayLee helped he felt important and close to his mom. Mom also collected ideas for easy, enjoyable things that BayLee could do alone.

Baylee's friend Branson with similar temperament also seems attracted to trouble. At 4, he discovered he could get his teacher's attention by touching girls' bodies or rolling on the floor to look under their dresses. Fortunately, his teacher knew about temperament. She knew that the more she tried to stop him directly, the more he would push this limit. So instead, she kept him busy. She encouraged him to play running games with the other boys. She gave him his own recess ball, because he got frustrated waiting for turns. When he rolled on the floor, she asked him to run an errand. And she talked alone with the girls about staying quietly clear of Branson. Because no one seemed to notice, Branson stopped testing this limit.

o **Weaning.** BayLee felt two very different ways about weaning. His active body didn't like staying in one place to nurse—he preferred to be up and moving. On the other hand, sucking calmed his body and made him feel safe. With days full of busy activities, he needed calm times for balance. He depended on Mom to help him with frustration; nursing helped to keep Mom nearby. Because nursing was important to BayLee, his mom made the change slowly. First, she dropped nursing after breakfast, then after lunch—times when he felt more independent. Rather than going to a cup, he went from nursing to bottles. Sucking is important to an active, easily frustrated child.

Words to Help Your Child Live with High Energy

Parent	Child
If you lovingly tell your child:	**Your child learns to say:**
You need lots of exercise each day.	*I need lots of exercise each day.*
You need a short break for some exercise.	*I need a short break for some exercise.*
Sometimes you think better when you're moving.	*Sometimes I think better when I'm moving.*
It's easier for you to sit if you move part of your body.	*It's easier for me to sit if I move part of my body.*

Words to Help Your Child Live with Frustration with Limits

See also Tarita Turtle, page 41.

Parent	Child
If you lovingly tell your child:	**Your child learns to say:**
Let's count while we wait.	*I'll count while I wait.*
Let's think of something fun (funny, etc.) instead.	*I'll think of something fun (funny, etc.) instead.*
In addition to this, what else would you really like right now?	*In addition to this, what else would I really like right now?*
Is there a way you can get part of what you want?	*Is there a way I can get part of what I want?*
What is something else that is sort of like what you want?	*What is something else that is sort of like what I want?*

BayLee Bluebird shares these behavior issues with other children in this book. For more help, see:

- Discipline, pp. 96–102.
- Eating out, pp. 63–64.
- Moodiness, page 55.
- Potty training, pp. 109–112.
- Sibling rivalry, pp. 112–114.
- Sleep, pp. 102–109.
- Tests limits and rules, pp. 46–47.

The Bear Cubs Temperament or Temperament Plus?

Imagine the darting speed of a bird, the intensity of a prowling tiger, and the powerful determination of a whale. When the temperaments of BayLee Bluebird, Tegan Tiger, and Walla Whale all combine, the result is the Olympic Challenge of Parenting. We call these human tornados the Bear Cubs. They are tossed by an internal storm of racing energy and a crowd of powerful feelings.

Both cubs are high in energy and intensity. They are also easily frustrated and slow to adapt. However, on other traits they are different. One cub, Commotion, is cautious. She hides behind Mom at birthday parties, resists swimming lessons, and won't hug Grandpa. Her brother, Comeback, is sensitive and very curious. He races off to explore all that is new, but screams if there is a tag in his shirt. His parents are forever calling, "Comeback!" Both cubs require a *lot of work* and they prove that there are different ways to be spirited. The cubs aren't *trying* to be difficult, but they repeatedly crash against the needs of others because 1) they have so much energy, 2) they are frustrated by both learning and limits, and 3) the more intense their feelings, the less they are able to adapt.

Hold your hats, everyone! You deserve the *gold medal* of parenting! Unfortunately, other adults rarely understand or appreciate the difficulty of your job. Take life one day at a time. Look back into the family tree. You may see traces of where some of these traits have come from.

Keys to Living with Many Challenging Traits

o **Plan ahead and step in early to *prevent* trouble.** Don't buy light-colored carpets. If possible, do your weekly shopping without taking the Bear Cubs. If Commotion has trouble putting shoes on, offer help before she gets upset, or let her go barefoot if shoes aren't really necessary. If Comeback has trouble peeling bananas, hand one to him already peeled. If the party is turning into a disaster, grab the twins and leave early.

Learning Style

Commotion and Comeback are active, intense, and easily frustrated. All people learn best when they feel calm and interested. Both Commotion and Comeback get discouraged and anxious when learning is difficult. In addition, curious Comeback is always thirsty for new things and quickly bored with the familiar. For him, the learning path is *narrow*—between anxiety on one side, and boredom on the other. Find activities and learning situations that suit his temperament. Focus on his current interests and build on his natural talents.

Common Behavior Issues

The Bear Cubs share many issues with three other children in this book—Tegan Tiger, Walla Whale, and BayLee Bluebird. See chapters 8, 9, and 10 for detailed help.

Many highly spirited preschoolers do beautifully as they grow into more self-control and as you discover the activities and environments that suit them. For others, the path is more complicated.

○ **Attention span is short.** Attention can shift because of high sensitivity to distractions, frustration with the task at hand, the need for exercise, or boredom. Slow to adapt children may seem inattentive because they are still thinking of the earlier topic.

The ability to pay attention changes and increases with age. It's helpful to think about three different kinds of attention. The first is attention to possible danger, as in a baby's startle reflex. The second is attention to personal interests. Some preschoolers ride their bikes round and round while others love puzzles, drawing, or make believe. The third is the ability to put one's attention where parents or teachers want it. It's not until age 6 or 7 that the needed neurons connect in many normal children. Historically, academic education started at 7 years. Today, some schools, and the world's most effective education systems, such as Finland's, follow the same pattern.

Fours don't clean up their rooms unless we're there to make it interesting because they don't yet have the third kind of attention. Similarly, many kindergartners have difficulty paying attention to the teacher. Today, unfortunately, many schools criticize young children for their lack of ability to pay attention to the interests of others. It's like criticizing them for being short. In most pre-schoolers, attention gradually increases as they explore activities that are *personally interesting.*

○ **ADHD or Attention Deficit Hyperactivity Disorder** affects about five to eight percent of children worldwide. These children are impulsive, highly active, and distractible. This includes some, *not all,* of the bear cubs. To qualify for diagnosis, these issues need to cause difficulty in two different environments, such as home and school. Before age 6, The American Academy of Pediatrics recommends behavior management as the best treatment. Medication is generally not recommended early on because, 1) many wild 4s grow into much more focused 7s and 2) the most effective medicines may have more side effects in the younger children. Because other conditions (including poor sleep, learning disabilities, stress, early trauma) can look like ADHD, careful evaluation is important.

○ **Can't cooperate or won't cooperate?** Some children appear difficult or rebellious even when they try their best. This may be because they struggle with subtle developmental delays or learning disabilities, from auditory processing, to dyslexia to high-functioning autism (formerly known as Asperger's syndrome). Children who are either quite high or low in sensitivity may have difficulty with sensory processing. If temperament management isn't helping, talk with doctors and teachers about further evaluation.

○ **Class clown.** When Comeback Bear Cub gets bored or discouraged he makes the other children laugh with his funny faces and jokes. That's more fun than boredom. It's less embarrassing than letting others see that he can't do what they can. To help, figure out what is too easy or too hard for him. The better the class material matches his ability and interests, the less he clowns around.

Trait combinations that add difficulty:

1) *Low sensitivity and low regularity:* With low awareness of body cues (tired, hungry), and unclear daily biorhythms, it takes more attention to manage rest and eating.

2) *Curious (or high energy) and slow to adapt:* Curiosity (as well as energy) pulls these children into new situations which then require adaptation. This causes an internal tug-of-war. Explain to your 4-year old, "You love new things and get frustrated that new things often come with new rules."

3) *Intense children who are low in energy:* They have strong feelings on the inside that don't show on the outside. They often feel misunderstood. Once they understand numbers, ask, "On a scale of 1 to 5, how disappointed are you?"

Your understanding of temperament and these management tools will help your child mature and enjoy childhood. Over time, children are more able to reach their maximum potential when they understand their own temperament. If you have further concerns, seek professional help along the way.

Shared Behavior Issues of Many Temperament Types

The issues of managing strong feelings, discipline, potty training, sibling rivalry, and sleep are common to many children in this book. Information is pulled together here by topic because approaches that help with other children may also help with yours.

How to Manage Strong Feelings

Biting and Hitting

Parents are often surprised when their children are aggressive. Children can be aggressive even though they don't see violence on the media or at home. Why? Tegan Tiger has strong feelings all through her body, including in her mouth. At 10 months, she sometimes gave Mom a happy hug and then bit Mom on the shoulder. Mom was always startled and yelped, "Ouch! That hurts!" She set Tegan down immediately, left the room, and counted slowly to ten. (See "chewelry" on line.)

At 2 years, Tegan bit her playmate not just once, but several times. Mom felt *really* embarrassed. Mom picked Tegan up and said firmly, "Bite food, not friends," and moved Tegan away for two minutes. Mom gave Tegan rubber toys to bite and found a plastic bracelet so Tegan always had something nearby to bite.

High energy BayLee loves to wrestle with Dad. Sometimes they play pretend biting games at home. Bay Lee wants to play the same game with his friends at school, but when he forgets that it's pretend and closes his mouth, he hurts his friends. The teacher asked Dad not to play biting games at home. Sometimes BayLee gets excited and hugs a friend too hard. The teacher has him practice "hug gently."

Quiet, adaptable Cam was bitten several times by Tegan. High energy Walla instinctively protected herself by yelling, hitting back, or calling the teacher. Cam just cried. So the teacher said, "Cam, you need to practice your big voice to keep yourself safe. Before someone bites you, shout, 'No bites!'" Cam practiced with his teacher and his parents. Soon, no one was biting Cam.

At 3, Tegan still hit other children at times. The teacher separated them calmly and firmly. She asked Tegan get a cool cloth for the hurt child and sit nearby until the other child felt better. Tegan could see how her actions affected others.

Fenson, an intense and sensitive 3-year-old, started a new preschool. The teacher reported that Fenson hit several children. Mom explained that Fenson gets overwhelmed with too much noise or when children crowd too close. The teacher helped Fenson find some quiet places where he could be alone when he needed peaceful space. She also taught him to hold his arms out straight and say, "Stop, I need this much space." As Fenson learned to protect his personal space, he hit less and less often.

BayLee is not only energetic and easily frustrated, he is also low in sensitivity. He has a high pain tolerance. He doesn't even notice bumps and bruises—he jumps right back up to play. When the teacher says, "Hitting hurts," he doesn't really understand. For several weeks one teacher followed him like a shadow. Whenever she saw trouble coming, she said, "BayLee, use your words." Things slowly got better.

Temper Tantrums

◑ Why and when?

When intense Tegan Tiger was a baby her parents always came to her rescue. Mom nursed her whenever she wanted calories or comfort. Dad carried her around when she was bored and rocked her to sleep. But gradually, after many months, her parents changed. They no longer gave her everything she wanted the moment she wanted it. Tegan cried because of this new distance between them and cried because she couldn't always have whatever she wanted as soon as she wanted it. She got mad! Her screams of protest were her first temper tantrums.

Pawly Puppy, with moderate temperament, first had tantrums at 2½ years. Mellow Cam Chameleon had a few mild tantrums at 3½. But intense Tegan Tiger started having tantrums—lots of them—at 14 months.

◑ Triggers and types of tantrums

What triggers tantrums in your house? List several causes. Triggers can help you decide how best to respond. It also helps to think of two different types of tantrums.

Manipulative Tantrums

Purpose: To control other people or their things

Cause: Wants and wishes—have a cookie, draw on the walls, watch another video, have a new toy, play with parent's computer

Parent action: Calmly and firmly hold the line to avoid spoiling

Temperament Tantrums

Purpose: To release emotional tension created by temperament (or made worse by being tired or hungry)

Causes: Is anxious in a new situation, has run out of adaptation energy, feels overloaded by too much stimulation or frustration, or needs exercise

Parent action: Plan ahead to avoid such tantrums in the future. This is respecting temperament, not "giving in" or spoiling.

o Track Tantrums

How often?
Once a week? Several a day? Tegan's mom also put an X on the calendar for each tantrum. Over time she could see that they gradually came less often.

How long to they last?
Pawly Puppy cries for two to three minutes, while intense Tegan Tiger screams for 30 to 40 minutes. Tegan's mom says to herself, "There goes the tiger's roar for 30 minutes." Because she knows what to expect, life feels more in control.

What is the intensity level?

Level 1. *Intensity beginning to rise.* Tegan frowns, stops making eye contact, gets a special "look" in her eyes; her voice gets louder or higher, she talks faster or may be unable to talk. At this point, her parents may be able to slow down, divert her attention, or find a compromise that prevents a *temperament* tantrum.

Level 2. *Meltdown.* Tegan screams, throws things, hits, kicks, and sometimes bites. At this point, tantrums run their course, like fireworks that flare in the sky until they fade.

○ Safety and positive practice

High energy BayLee may hit and kick, bite or throw things during tantrums. Mom holds him to keep everyone safe, including herself. She pulls him onto her lap, facing away from her so he can't bite. She holds BayLee's arms over his belly button so he can't hit. She holds her head to the side so he can't smack her face with his head. Mom spreads her legs or puts one leg across his legs so he can't kick. BayLee yells, but no one gets hurt. Mom says, "I need to hold you until you can be a safe boss of your body." (When Tegan's dad couldn't hold Tegan because of his broken arm, he stepped into the bathroom and locked the door for several minutes.)

Intense 2s get a powerful surge of energy when angry. They need safe ways to release this energy. Dad taught Tegan to stomp and growl. Mom taught BayLee to clasp his hands together and shake them. When in a good mood, they practice the angry game: "Let's pretend we're happy, 'Ha, Ha.'" "Let's pretend we are sad, 'Boo Hoo.'" "Let's pretend we are angry, 'GRRRRR (stomp, stomp).'" When Tegan gets upset and hits a friend, Mom separates her and has Tegan practice "stomp and growl" three times before she returns to play. Aunt Trina complained that stomp and growl wasn't very civilized. Dad answered, "It's better that hitting or biting. No one gets hurt and there are no mean words." Alternative ways to release angry energy include hit a punching bag, jump up and down, and hit or kick a pillow. With time and practice, Tegan and BayLee each learned to be "a safe boss of my body."

○ Regaining control

Children calm down in different ways. Distraction works for some. Some settle most quickly when held, some if the parent stays nearby (in sight, but not touching), and others with parents out of sight. Some first need time by themselves and later a hug.

Mom put Tegan on the sofa for time-out so Tegan could scream and kick without hurting anyone. Unlike Pawly Puppy, Tegan jumped right off. The patio didn't work either. So Mom took Tegan to her room. She said, "If you stay in your room, I'll leave the door open. If you come out, I'll close the door." When Tegan was 2, time-out was two minutes. When Taiga turned 4, Mom could say, "You can come out when you are a safe boss of your body." Tegan occasionally stormed out too soon. Mom calmly repeated the goal: "You can come out when you are a safe boss of your body. We'll try again." (Some parents stand and hold the door shut if needed while others lock the door—one minute per year. When Tegan threw toys, the toys went to the toy jail for an hour.)

Tantrums really upset Tegan's parents. When Tegan had strong feelings so did Mom. Mom used to say to herself, "Tegan is *so difficult!*" or, "Why can't I be more patient?" She felt anger, blame, or guilt. In order to avoid a spiral of intensity, Mom needed ways to stay calm. Wearing ear plugs helps her during long tantrums. She's also learned to say different things to herself during Tegan's tantrums, such as, "Life is tough when you are 2," or, "Big feelings are hard for small kids." With less blame and guilt it is easier for Mom to stay calm.

When Tegan screams in a store, Mom waits or she carries Tegan away from the crowd or to the car. When strangers give angry looks, Mom says to herself, "If you had a child like Tegan, you would understand!" Dad carries a sign he can clip to his pocket that reads, "Temper Tantrum in Progress—not to worry."

Build Emotional Intelligence

Not surprisingly, it takes years for intense Tegan to learn how to manage her strong feelings. Her parents help step by step.

- **Name feelings.** (2 years and up) Teach by naming the feelings you see: You look sad, disappointed, frustrated, scared, etc. Children who understand words like dinosaur and refrigerator can understand the names of feelings.

- **Calm down.** (3 years and up) Practice ways to calm down: A break? A hug? Blow out imaginary candles? For lots of options, see "Self-Calming Cards" from www.ParentingPress.com. Role play anger management tools (including stomp and growl).

- **Describe feelings.** (3 years and up) "I hear your feelings are getting big because you are talking louder." Talk about big feelings *after the fact*: "You were really mad when you threw the truck!" or "You were excited when you splashed water out of the tub," or "You were happy when you hugged your cousin so hard she cried."

  Around 4, find an image your child likes. How about a pot of water that is cool, warm, or boiling? Or the flame of a candle, flame in the fireplace, or a big fire? A fire engine resting in the station or racing to a fire? A breeze versus a thunderstorm, small or large waves at the beach? A resting or angry dinosaur? A bus, train, or race horse? One 5-year-old described her feelings as a volcano. Help children notice when feelings are starting to get bigger or faster. "Are you feeling wound up? Revved up? How fast is your engine running? How big is your flame? What could help your train slow down?" Praise children for noticing and describing their intensity.

○ **Measure feelings.** (4 years and up) As children understand numbers, get more specific: On a scale of 1 to 5 or 1 to 10 (from calm to out of control): "How big are your feelings right now? How happy are you? How sad?" Around age 5, ask children to notice how *big a feeling is,* and then *how important the issue is.* Tegan's intense feelings are almost always 9 or 10. But at age 5, she could begin to see that some things were more *important* than others. Breaking her favorite doll was a 10, but spilling milk on her shirt was only a 3. That helped her get a grip on some of her feelings.

○ **Understand feelings.** (4 years and up) Once the dust settles, 4s are able to learn three important things about feelings.

1) What we do with feelings affects what happens next. In Elizabeth Crary's book, *I'm Frustrated,* children choose what to do next, then turn to a different page to see the outcome.

2) Anger is a secondary emotion. Anger comes after another feeling, such as disappointment, fear, loneliness, feeling unloved, or unfairly treated. To help Tegan learn these important underlying feelings, her mom said, "You were really mad at BayLee today. I wonder if you were disappointed that he wouldn't play with you." (If 4s can't talk about their *own* feelings, role play feelings with stuffed animals.)

3) Thoughts create feelings, rather than vice versa. Tegan sees a big package with a fancy bow. If she thinks it's for her, she'll feel excited. If she thinks it's not for her, she'll feel disappointed. Encourage 4s to think back slowly to what they thought just *before* a big feeling came up. Understanding underlying feelings makes problem solving easier.

○ **Solve problems.** (4 years and up) This set of questions paves the way to problem solving:

1) "What happened, Tegan?" ("Baylee wouldn't play with me.")

2) "What did you think—or what did you worry about?" ("That I'd have to play all by myself.")

3) "What did you do?" ("I hit him.")

4) "What could you do next time that would work better?" ("Find someone else to play with, or tell the teacher I'm lonely.")

Discipline

With easy children, parents tell them what to do once or twice and they do it. Not so when children are high in energy, slow to adapt, or easily frustrated. Here, teaching and learning appropriate behavior is hard work and takes years to accomplish.

Before BayLee could crawl, Mom and Dad supported his new adventures. Mom clapped when he first rolled over and Dad smiled when BayLee first held a cup. But once he could crawl, Mom and Dad would frown or get upset with some new adventures. When he wanted to play in the kitty litter, they put it out of reach. They wouldn't let him crawl in the dusty fireplace, taste dust balls from under the sofa, or munch crackers he found on the sidewalk. Surely there is a mistake. BayLee thought, "I'll try that fireplace again to see if they clap or smile this time." They don't. His purpose wasn't to challenge their authority. He simply has many new things to learn about life.

When Dad said, "Move," he expected Walla to move! Mom expected Walla to leave her toys on a moment's notice to get in the car. But Walla didn't. Her parents didn't know that a sudden, strong "Go!" or "Stop!" *increases Walla's intensity and lowers her flexibility.* Then it's harder for her to cooperate, even if she wants to. Walla had one temper tantrum after another. Everyone was miserable. Gradually, her parents understood that Walla can't change quickly. She always needs time to change the picture in her mind before she can change her body.

BayLee tries to avoid the frustration of accepting a limit by pushing past it. His attention locks in on what he wants. He asks or goes after it again, and again, and again. At some point, all his "wanting" energy shifts from wanting to climb on the counter to pushing past the barrier, which is often Mom or Dad. At first, his parents didn't stand firm in these storms. They changed their mind and gave in. BayLee learned to push harder to get his way. As his parents learned to make better choices about discipline, BayLee learned that pushing harder didn't work.

Ways to Make Discipline Easier

- **Sleep and food.** Sleep restores adaptation energy and frustration tolerance for both adults and children. Similarly, hunger can cause more resistance. Consider the need for rest and nutrition, especially if children have irregular body rhythms.

- **Good relationship.** Ideally spend 10 to 20 minutes each day (sometimes called "time-in") building a positive relationship. Because parents, necessarily, make so many daily decisions, spend this time doing what the *child* wants to do. (Reading doesn't count because the *book* takes over the interaction.) Mom or Dad copies BayLee, as they play follow-the-leader, or draw, or build. If they play with cars, Dad takes the smaller, slower car. Children need five to seven positive interactions for each correction during the day. Time-in helps bank positive interactions.

○ **Enforce rules calmly.** When Mom is calm, BayLee can pay attention to the problem, rather than being distracted by *Mom's feelings.* (Pretend you are in a stage play, in the role of your calmest friend.) You are also modeling the anger management you want your child to learn.

○ **Expect BayLee to test the rules.** When BayLee throws a block, Dad says to himself, "Just like I expected, he's checking to see if the rule has gone away." Because Dad wasn't surprised or disappointed, it was easier for Dad to stay calm while he took the blocks away.

○ **Learning curve.** Because Walla is slow to adapt, it often takes a week or so to learn a new rule. Walla was used to jumping on the old living room sofa. When they got a new sofa, Mom needed to take her off it 12 times and calmly put her on her own bed to jump. Walla finally has a mind picture that the new sofa was for reading on, not jumping on.

○ **Grant wishes in fantasy.** Once BayLee turned 4, Mom used a new approach. When BayLee demanded ice cream in the car, Mom said, "If you *did* have an ice cream, what flavor would it be?"

○ **Give opportunities for control.** Let BayLee and Walla make choices when it's safe and reasonable: Which shirt to wear? Which park to play in? Which friend to play with? Follow them in a game of follow-the-leader, and say, "Now it's your turn to be the boss." However, don't give more choices than they can handle.

Because Baylee has so much energy, it's easy for his parents to switch between too many rules and too few. When parents come home tired from work, Grandma is ill, and the roof is leaking, life is too busy! Mom and Dad are too worn out to enforce the rules. BayLee gets out of control. Mom and Dad get overwhelmed by all his noise and trouble. They react with anger and punishment, saying "No!" to everything. Now, having been angry and harsh, they feel guilty and back off. BayLee gets out of control again, and the whole cycle starts all over.

Hoping to avoid tantrums, Tegan's parents give in more than they want to. Tegan then pushes more and more. Suddenly her parents are angry and resentful. They get too tough and demanding, then feel guilty, give in, and the cycle begins again.

Inconsistent parenting means the rules keep changing. It is as though red means "stop" one day, and "go" the next. Children get confused and have to keep testing the rules to see what they are right now. To get out of this pattern, set realistic limits sooner before you get angry. There will be a mighty protest at first. However, rules that stay the same are easier to remember. Also, work on only a couple of issues at a time so you have the energy to be consistent.

There is a special risk for parents of a spirited child. The more one parent gets angrily firm, the more the other gets loose and accepting. Both parents are looking for balance within the family. The child is content to go to whomever gives in. However, this pattern is extremely hard on couple relationships because each sees the other as harming the child. Instead, try "I'll support you on this if you'll support me on that." If disagreements continue, get professional help. Your job is not an easy one.

Teach Better Behavior

When active BayLee hears Mom yell "No!" he often doesn't know what he *should do* instead. Active BayLee gets into more things than low energy children do. Can he climb the living room bookshelf or open the kitchen drawers to make a stairway to the counter top? Some parents set *too many* limits because they don't understand how much he needs to move. Other parents set *too few* limits because they get overwhelmed or because they felt over-controlled when they were young. Aim for the middle ground.

- **Choose your battles.** Make a *short* list of important rules and stick to them. Examples might be: "Use your words, touch gently." "Stay in your room at bedtime." "Food stays in the kitchen." Some problems go away if you ignore them. A toddler will only bang the cupboard door so many times before moving on to something else.

- **Say what the child can do.** BayLee is allergic to "No" and "Don't." Instead of "Don't run in the street," say, "Hold my hand in the street." Children's minds work in pictures. When you say "Don't throw sand," the picture they see is, "Throw sand." Paint word pictures of what *you want them to do: "Pour the sand."* Two yeses are even better: "You can drop the sand or pour the sand." "Use the step stool or ask for help" (rather than use the drawers as stairs to the counter).

- **Two yeses and a consequence.** The process is even stronger with three parts. "You can pour water or splash water in the tub. If water goes out of the tub bath time is over." "You can *talk* to the dog or *pet* the dog gently. If you hit him, I'll put him outside." If the same issue keeps coming up, take some time to figure out all three parts.

- **Practice desired behavior.** At 2, and 3, BayLee sometimes hit others when he was angry. After he hit someone, and after he calmed down, Mom had him practice "stomp and growl" three times before he did anything else. It helped him remember what to do next time. Once he was 4, she had him practice the words he could have used instead of hitting.

- **Red, green or yellow light?** Red light rule: the car doesn't move until everyone is buckled in. Green light: play with Legos®. Those two rules are easy. Yellow lights are the problem if it's sometimes "yes" and sometimes "no," like sweets, or screen time. Without clarity, Walla *has* to keep asking. Set clear rules, such as sweets at dinner or only on weekends. Set when and how much screen time.

- **Let me think about it.** When Walla asks for something unexpected, Mom says, "I need a minute (or an hour or a day) to decide." Better to think it through than to change later. Once you are sure of the answer, it will be easier to stand firm if there is a stormy reaction.

- **Plan ahead.** Mom and Dad have learned to tell Walla about new rules *ahead of time,* whenever possible. The less rules surprise her, the less they upset her. Walla strongly resists some new rules at first. Once they are part of her mind picture, she *likes* rules and routines. The more she knows what will happen next, the more secure and relaxed she feels.

- **Family Meetings.** At 4 years, weekly family meetings are helpful. Review the up-coming week, talk about outings, discuss and brainstorm issues. Adjust rules when needed. Life goes more smoothly with added clarity and fewer surprises.

Avoid and Stop Trouble

- **Avoid unnecessary temptations.** Childproof, childproof, childproof. Don't take busy BayLee to the antique store. Want to avoid a meltdown because of candy at the checkout stand? Mom shopped alone or went early in the day when BayLee is more able to handle frustration. No leisurely meals in fancy restaurants unless BayLee is home with a sitter.

- **Be the brakes he doesn't yet have.** A small car does fine with small brakes, but Baylee is in a steam engine. It takes years before his brakes grow strong enough to stop him. Thank goodness, Mother Nature made parents bigger than children. Restrain or carry BayLee when needed.

- **Redirect.** BayLee's curiosity is useful in the early years. When he reaches for something dangerous, Dad can easily distract him with something else.

- **Touch, don't move.** BayLee is a kinesthetic learner—learns more by touching than seeing or hearing. Pushing too hard against his natural instincts can backfire into rebellion. At 2, Mom held Grandmother's vase so he could safely touch it. At 3, Dad taught him that he could touch things in stores if he didn't *move* them. He could satisfy his curiosity without destroying the store.

- **Time-out.** This can give everyone a needed break—one minute per year. Time-out can be on the sofa, or in the child's room with door open or closed. It depends on where the child will stay put. In some families, it's easier if the *parent* steps away briefly into a bedroom or bathroom. Slowly counting 1-2-3 before time-out gives Walla time to shift and stop a problem behavior like teasing her cousin.

How to Get Things Done

BayLee gets easily frustrated or bored so he quits things that aren't interesting or important to him—like getting dressed in the morning.

- **Simplify.** Put school clothes on the night before—most children in the world don't wear pajamas. Take a jacket along and let BayLee put it on when he gets cold. Tired of so many toys on the floor? Divide them into three boxes. Put two out of reach, and rotate the boxes once a month.

○ **Work together.** BayLee is a people person. Working with others helps him stay on track, He brushes teeth, gets dressed, picks up toys, makes beds with one of his parents.

○ **Work before pleasure.** Get dressed before breakfast, pick up toys before screen time. This way, BayLee has a reason to finish the task. Put his shoes and socks in the car. He'll have more incentive to put them on in order to get *out* of the car. (He doesn't have personal reasons to get *in* the car because that means sitting still and soon leaving parents for the day.)

Match this approach to your child's interests. If Dad wants to get out and low energy Tarita doesn't, there's no point in saying, "If you don't pick up your toys we won't go out." Don't punish the parent more than the child.

○ **Transition time.** See "Plan ahead," page 60 for ways to ease transitions.

○ **Picture list.** At 2½, post a picture list of the morning and evening routines.

○ **Ask, don't tell.** At 4 years, don't bother to tell BayLee the rules he already knows. Instead, ask, "How do we talk in the library?" or, "What do you need to do before bedtime story?" Instead of brushing off your nagging, he has to *think* about the answer.

○ **Choice.** "Do you want to walk or be carried to bed (to the car)?" "Do you want to pick up the blocks or the crayons?" If Tegan slows down during clean-up, Mom moves more slowly, too.

○ **Winning.** This is an effective incentive for some children. "Who can get dressed first?" "Who can get to the car first?"

○ **Waiting.** The car doesn't start until seat belts are buckled. Eating starts after hands are washed. If Walla won't help pick up toys, she has to sit on the sofa (without any toys) while Mom silently picks them up. "I can't talk. I'm thinking about toys to pick up."

○ **Consequences to get things done.** Set a timer for the *end* of nightly story hour—not the beginning. The sooner teeth get brushed and pajamas are on, the more time there is for stories.

○ **Contracts.** At 4 years, contracts are useful because children this age can think about problems and solve them. Besides, contracts are planned ahead and that suits Walla. Mom asked, "Should we pick up your toys before or after dinner? "After dinner because I'm not so hungry," Walla said. "What if they aren't all picked up in five minutes?" Walla couldn't think of a consequence so Mom said, "Then I'll put leftover toys out of reach for a week." Walla protested. They agreed that toys would go away for two days.

○ **Star charts are also helpful starting at 3 years.** At 4, stars become points toward bigger rewards, such as an extra story, an outing with parents, or art supplies, etc.

Sleep

Getting to Bed

○ **Too excited for bed.** With active BayLee, parents have learned that he needs about two hours of "slowdown time" before bed. Otherwise, he's too excited to sleep. For BayLee, baths are fun and exciting. Because the family gets home late, they just give baths on weekends. And Dad only plays chase on weekends. When the family goes out for dinner on Saturday, they go early so they can be home two hours before bedtime. Every child is different. Other high energy children find baths are soothing, and some shift from running to sleeping as soon as they hit the mattress.

Sensitive, intense Fenson Fawn is upset by people in his personal space, so baths and dressing are not relaxing. His parents plan 30 minutes of low level activity, songs, and stories between bath and bedtime.

○ **Getting ready for bed.** BayLee never hears when Dad calls, "It's time to go to bed." So instead, Dad touches his shoulder, looks him in the eye and says, "When the timer rings, it will be time to get ready for bed." When the timer rings, Dad sets it again for the *end* of story time. The sooner BayLee gets in bed, the more time is left for stories before the timer rings again. BayLee and Dad then brush their teeth together and Dad helps him into his pajamas. BayLee Bluebird does better with a team effort. It doesn't matter that other children his age can get ready for bed by themselves.

○ **The bedtime ritual.** Like most of his friends, BayLee loves the same bedtime ritual. When BayLee was 2, Dad had to read the *same* story night after night. Dad was *really* bored, but the same familiar story helps calm a restless mind and body. Any tiny change in the evening ritual caused upset, protest, and more difficulty falling asleep.

Places to Sleep

Where is the best place for children to sleep in the early years? Wherever the whole family gets the most sleep.

o **Parent's bed.** After outgrowing a bedside co-sleeper or bassinet, some babies move into the parental bed. That's safer if the bed is on the floor and more comfortable if the bed is large.

o **Child's room.** From the beginning, Mom wanted to sleep in the same room as BeiShu (BayLee's cousin). But sensitive BeiShu woke whenever Mom moved or Dad snored. Mom, who was also sensitive, woke whenever BeiShu sniffled. They moved BeiShu to her own room. They used a white noise machine to help block out neighborhood sounds and put black-out curtains on her windows.

At 5 months, moderate temperament Pawly was moved to her own room when she started nursing less often during the night.

At 11 months, active Walla climbed out of her crib. Dad put the crib mattress on the floor, and later they bought a toddler bed. They childproofed the room carefully. For safety, they needed her to stay in her room and they knew she could climb over a baby gate. They tried two gates, one on top of the other, then decided to close the door with a childproof lock on the inside knob.

Once slow to adapt Tegan was in a toddler bed, she came to Mom's room during the night. Mom decided to sleep on sofa pillows in Tegan's room until Tegan was comfortable in her new bed.

o **Musical beds.** As an active toddler, Walla went to sleep most quickly when Mom snuggled with Walla in her toddler bed. Mom was exhausted so she often fell asleep before Walla did. Even after she was asleep, Walla wiggled and kicked so much that Mom couldn't sleep for long. Mom left to go sleep with Dad. Later Walla woke and came to their bed. That was too crowded for Dad so he left to sleep in hers. When Walla turned 3, she slept more easily on her own.

Midnight move to parent's bed. When intense Tegan woke during the night, she came to her parents' bed. As she was so quiet, and her parents sound sleepers, they often didn't notice until they woke in the morning. Because Tegan began every night in her own bed, she gradually slept there longer and came to her parents' bed less often.

Midnight move to a mat. Because BayLee rolled and kicked so much in his sleep, his parents did *not* want him in their bed. They put a mat on the floor by their bed. Mom explained, "If you come here quietly you can sleep beside our bed. If you wake me up, I'll need to take you back to your bed because I need my sleep." After some difficult nights when Mom took BayLee back to his bed repeatedly, he learned to stay quiet on the mat. After some months, his parents gradually moved the mat a little farther from their bed, closer to their door, and then just outside their door.

Getting Enough Sleep

Easily frustrated BayLee needs a full night's sleep to handle tomorrow's frustrations. Slow to adapt Tegan needs a full night's sleep to refill her tank of adaptation energy. Life is better for everyone when these children get enough sleep.

When moderate temperament Pawly gets tired, she just falls asleep. Not so for other children. When BayLee gets over-tired, his engine speeds up. When Tegan gets too tired, her intensity goes up. Neither child can go to sleep! When they are over-tired and can't get to sleep until late, parents have to wake them in the morning. They start the next day sleep-deprived. Without enough sleep, the next day is filled with resistance, fussing, and frantic energy on BayLee's part. No wonder it can take days to straighten things out again.

Seeing that BayLee was over-tired, his parents started evening slowdown and the bedtime ritual 15 minutes earlier. After three days, they moved it another 15 minutes earlier and repeated the process. After two weeks, BayLee was waking up on his own in the morning. The days became much easier. Several months later, he again became over-tired. So on Saturday, they made sure he got plenty of extra exercise in the afternoon. That evening, they started evening slowdown and the bedtime ritual early. Again, his behavior and mood improved the next day. During holidays, BayLee and Tegan get so excited, they need extra time to calm down before bed. Their parents start the evening slowdown and bedtime a little early. At times of stress, as when Grandpa is sick or when starting a new school, it's especially important for BayLee and Tegan to get enough sleep.

Falling Asleep

O **Irregualr body rhythms.** If your baby is irregular and adapts easily, pay attention to the *child,* not the *clock,* to determine sleep time. Put her down when her eyes droop. If she is also slow to adapt, a scheduled bedtime becomes helpful over time. You provide a regular routine. She falls asleep when tired. Let her look at books or listen to soft music while waiting to fall asleep.

o **4-month fallout.** At 4 months moderate temperament Pawly suddenly began to have trouble getting to sleep at night. Her day had been so interesting, it was hard to slow down! Mom and Dad changed to calm activities before bedtime rather than swings in the air with Dad. They set a regular bedtime routine—bath, snuggling, and songs. Soon, Pawly was falling asleep easily again. Pawly usually sleeps well. However, when she's teething, or her schedule changes because of vacations or exciting visitors, she needs extra help to settle down.

o **Frustration and sleep cues.** The longer easily frustrated children like Tarita Turtle or BayLee Bluebird lie awake and alone, the more frustrated they get. Sometimes their bodies get so tense that they *can't* fall asleep. Children who are easily frustrated normally want company while falling asleep. They're more dependent at the end of the day and especially at bedtime.

At bedtime, Mom usually snuggled for 30 minutes in Tarita's room. Tarita fell asleep stroking Mom's hair. Mom was Tarita's bridge into sleep. Not surprisingly, Tarita had great difficulty falling asleep when Mom was out for the evening. Mom knew that sleep cues, or physical signals for sleep, are important. When Tarita turned 3, Mom said, "We are going to a store that sells cloth. We will find a piece of cloth that feels like my hair." In the store, they found several pieces of soft cloth. Mom told Turtia to close her eyes and say which felt most like Mom's hair. Mom sat beside Tarita's bed for several nights while Tarita stroked her new "mommy hair."

o **Fall asleep on the run.** For BayLee, it's hard to lie still long enough to fall asleep. Active babies find rhythmic motion is more soothing than lying still. As a baby, nursing and rocking did the trick. Mom's breasts got sore and Dad spelled her off with a pacifier and a bottle. Not surprisingly, other youngsters gave up night feedings before BayLee. Eventually, Mom shortened night nursings and then cut them out one by one. Because a bottle of milk could be a problem for his teeth, Dad gradually diluted the milk with more water—just an ounce at a time so BayLee couldn't tell the difference. Because BayLee could now move around in his bed, Dad also clipped several pacifiers (on very short ribbons) in his crib so BayLee could find them during the night. They allowed a pacifier only in bed because they wanted BayLee to practice talking during the day.

When Baylee turned 3, the dentist said that so much sucking could harm the position of BayLee's teeth. Mom looked for other kinds of soothing. She made up a quiet stretching song which she sang more and more slowly. BayLee first stretched each arm and then each leg. When BayLee turned 4, Mom suggested that he sing the stretching song to himself or listen to a recorded story that was calm and familiar. Usually, BayLee was then able to get to sleep by himself. When life is more frustrating, BayLee sometimes needs help to fall asleep—especially during an illness and after the family moved.

○ **Parent connections.** When Fenson turned 2, he complained about going to sleep in his room. He said he missed Mommy and Daddy. Dad put pictures of Mom and Dad on Fenson's wall and talked about a ribbon of love that always connects people who love each other. This helped Fenson go to sleep more easily.

○ **Schedule problem.** When active Walla was 4, she resisted bedtime and lay awake for an hour or more before falling asleep. She got to sleep so late that Mom had to wake her every morning. Mom asked at preschool, "Can she nap earlier in the day?" "Can you wake her after just a short nap?" "Can you skip her nap?" The preschool said no. Mom found another school with a better schedule for Walla. Without an afternoon nap, Walla easily went to bed at an earlier time and woke up rested. She no longer needed an afternoon nap.

○ **Mind in motion.** At 3, Dad helped Fenson plan quiet things to think about while falling asleep—a cloud floating in the sky or a spaceship sliding past stars. At 4, Mom noticed that at bedtime, Fenson often talked about worries. He couldn't get them out of his head. What about the argument he had with his best friend? Would he spill his milk again? Mom put an envelope by his bedside that said "Better Ways." She wrote his worry on a piece of paper and put it in the envelope. She said, "Your worry is right here so you don't have to think about it anymore tonight. Tomorrow we'll look and see what ideas you have for a better way to think about it, or to take care of it." Fenson was surprised that he often *did* have a better idea in the morning. Even if he didn't, he had gotten to sleep more easily. In time, Fenson could simply imagine putting worries into a "Better Way" envelope for the next day.

○ **End of an intense day.** For intense Tegan, it is hard to fall asleep when muscles are tense. When Tegan was a baby, Mom rocked, sang, and gave baby massage. When she was a toddler, it became

Dad's job to put her to bed. Tegan didn't want to be left alone. She cried. Dad felt bad. He stayed and patted. Tegan stayed awake to be sure he didn't leave. As the months went by, she begged for *more* stories. Dad's heart ached for her and he read more stories. The more she learned to talk, the better her reasons were for him to stay. Gradually, the bedtime ritual got longer and longer. The later she got to bed, the more tired she was, and the more difficulty she had getting to sleep. Bedtime became a disaster.

Finally, they decided that Mom would put Tegan to bed because she could stay firm and calm. Mom also knew that because Tegan is slow to adapt, she would resist any change at first. But she also knew that Tegan felt anxious when routines kept changing. Mom settled on a plan she could live with and told Tegan about it ahead of time: a hug, one story, and a back rub for five minutes. Then Mom would stay in the room and read, check emails, or do some yoga.

If Tegan talked to her, Mom did not answer because it was time for Tegan to rest. If Tegan got out of bed, Mom left the room and left the door open. If Tegan left the room, Mom put her back inside and closed the door until Tegan yelled that she was back in bed. When Tegan said she needed to use the potty, Mommy brought the potty into her room. She wouldn't let Tegan go to the bathroom. Tegan yelled and complained, but after five nights she knew that Mom wasn't going to change her mind. The next night, and thereafter, she went to sleep without any fuss. Dad was amazed! Mom was glad she knew about temperament, and that a very regular routine is the friend of a slow to adapt child.

Waking During the Night

o **Sleep cycles.** All children (and adults) have sleep cycles—falling asleep, deep sleep, dreams, then waking or almost waking. By 3 years, cycles usually last about 1½ hours and repeat through the night. Because BayLee wiggles so much, he wakes completely between many of his sleep cycles. Dad put up a night light in his room so he can see where he is when he wakes.

o **Hunger.** Pawly's mom knew that babies don't wake because they are hungry, but rather, when they wake between sleep cycles they may notice they are hungry. Babies have short sleep cycles (just 40 minutes) so they wake often. Mom also knew that babies gradually learn to take in more of their calories during the day instead of at night. Once Pawly weighed 15 pounds, Mom gradually shortened one nursing at a time and then dropped it. Moderate temperament Pawly then adjusted by taking those calories in during the day. Soon, Pawly was going to bed at 7 p.m., and waking for a feeding at 11 p.m., not long after Mom had gone to bed. So Mom gave a dream feed at 10 p.m.—silently offering the breast to Pawly in a dark room. Mom could then sleep till 2 a.m. Several months later, she shortened and then cut out the 2 a.m. feeding.

○ **High sensitivity.** When Fenson was a baby, he cried harder when Mom walked into his room and picked him up! Sensitive youngsters often feel surprised and upset when their personal space is suddenly invaded. Mom learned to stand nearby and sing or talk for a moment, stroke him, and finally pick him up.

○ **High activity.** At 7 to 8 months, many active babies start waking during the night. At first, active Walla woke up because now that she could roll both ways, she would smack into the sides of the crib. Several months later, Walla seemed to wake and think, "This is a great time to practice sitting, crawling, or standing." Mom moved the crib to Walla's own room so Mom could sleep better while Walla practiced.

○ **Development.** Babies get ready for crawling both physically and mentally. Mother Nature prepares the brain by building faster connections to the fear center of the brain, in case babies come across danger as they crawl. Their brains become wired to pay more attention to where Mom is, and thus babies are upset when she's not in sight. This is the phase of separation anxiety, and for a few weeks it may be harder for some babies to settle themselves at night.

○ **Nightmares.** BayLee sometimes has bad dreams. He cried during the night and for a while was afraid to be alone in his room. Mommy said that people sometimes see videos in their minds when they are asleep. They are called dreams. She asked about the story in his video. Bay Lee said Mommy is on the other side of a river in a storm, or that a monster is chasing him and he can't find her. Because of BayLee's temperament, he depends on Mom more than other children. BayLee is very afraid of losing her. (Of course, when the household is stormy with anger, parents can seem a little monster-like to small children.)

After a nightmare, Mom says,"Tell me the video story but with a nice ending." When he retells the story, the monster sometimes wants to play or is hungry so BayLee feeds him. Mom reassures

BayLee that she loves him. They talk about ways BayLee can ask for help, and things he can do while waiting for Mom. After Grandpa died, Mom hugged BayLee and told him, "I'm going to live a *long, long* time."

o **Cries when wakes in the morning.** Sensitive, intense Fenson cried briefly in the morning for several months even though life was going fairly smoothly. Dad said, "I need my morning coffee and he needs a morning fuss." When Fenson turned 3, Mom started bringing him a morning snack. She didn't say a word—just left it by his bed and gave him the time he needed to wake up slowly. He did better with time and something in his stomach.

Potty Training

Getting Ready

Potty training often is earlier and easier with children who have moderate temperaments. As they usually have regular body rhythms, it can be easier to catch a poop in the potty. On the other hand, active children may resist sitting for more than a moment. Slow to adapt children find it hard to drop what they are doing and rush to the potty. Easily frustrated ones may prefer that parents continue to take care of diapers. Few children potty train when there is a new baby around or there is other stress or change.

Readiness incudes interest in watching others, flushing, or sitting for a moment. Many children try out the potty long before they are ready to take on the day-in and day-out commitment. Expect two steps forward and one step back. Be prepared to back off for several months in between. Most children manage one part at a time, either pee or poop first.

Steps Along the Way

Around 2 years, support body awareness. When you see that special stance, announce in a friendly way, "Your pee-pee (or poop) is coming out."

Later, Tegan Tiger showed some interest and Mom wanted to clarify what was going on. On their way to the bathroom, her parents said, "I feel right here (pointing low in front or low in back) the pee (or poop) wants to come out so I'm going to let it go into the toilet." When emptying Tegan's diaper, Dad puts the poop in the potty chair (before the toilet). He says, "This is where your poops can go. The potty loves poops. It will be nice when you can let your poops go in the potty."

Children who are low in sensitivity are less aware of feelings both *outside* and *inside* their bodies. They aren't bothered by messy or wet diapers, especially because modern diapers feel so dry. Some parents increase awareness by switching to cotton training pants, putting training pants under diapers, or training when the child can go naked for some days or up to a week, so it is really obvious what is going on.

At some point, encourage your child to sit for a few minutes on the potty each day, when naked, such as upon waking in the morning or before or after a bath. The goal is simply to get comfortable with the potty, not to pee or poop in it. Some children love sitting naked and others may feel more comfortable with a towel over their lap. Enjoy this time. Sit nearby and talk or look at books, including some potty books.

To help Walla Whale, a natural planner, get the idea, Mom gave her a little cup of water to pour between her legs. She said, "The potty loves water and it loves pee, too." One day Mom also gave her three raisins to drop between her legs while she sat.

Many a parent has seen their child's quiet pause when a poop is about to plop into a diaper. Many a parent has rushed such a child to the bathroom. Unfortunately, when they get there, nothing happens. To the parent's frustration, the poop comes 10 minutes later, after *leaving* the bathroom. Why does this happen? Pooping is a complicated process that uses three sets of muscles. The intestines automatically move the poop along, the abdominal muscles may automatically tighten to push it out, yet the anus has to *relax and open*. For many children, especially those who are intense or cautious, their *entire* body tightens up when stressed.

Instead of rushing this child to the bathroom, simply say, "I see the poop is coming." Remind, "The potty loves poop!" Even when children notice the urge and willingly sit on the potty, it often takes a few minutes for the muscles to coordinate. Slow deep breaths can help. A natural way to encourage deep breaths is to talk or sing. Settle in for some comfortable talking and singing together.

Mom asked cautious Fenson Fawn, "Do you want to wear diapers or big boy pants this morning?" Gradually, Fenson chose big boy pants more often.

Some children do better with a schedule in the beginning. Slow to adapt children have trouble stopping what they are doing. Children who are low in sensitivity may not notice the need until it's too late to get to the potty in time. For these children it may work better to have regular routines, such as a potty stop after eating and before leaving the house or before getting in the car.

When Tegan was 2³/₄ Mom looked for a preschool that would accept her if she wasn't trained by 3. She knew it was better to be patient than to get into a battle.

For a time, Tegan stayed dry in her panties and asked for a diaper for poops. Then she went behind the sofa to poop. Mom made a new rule: "The bathroom is for pooping." She didn't pressure her to use the toilet, just to be in the bathroom to poop. Gradually Mom loosened her diaper, and eventually put it under the potty seat. At bedtime, Mom had Tegan imagine going to the bathroom, sitting on the potty, and pooping. She could practice without any pressure. After a week, Tegan pooped in the potty. (Some parents cut a hole in the diaper.)

With low sensitivity children, some parents train outside in the summer (or use part of the house with easy to clean floors), with a potty, a naked child, and lots of juice.

Resistance

Resistance usually means the child isn't ready. It's time to take another break. But there can be other reasons.

Some children find it hard to sit and poop. Squatting is more natural. Put the diaper on the floor to poop in as a transition step. When they switch to the potty or toilet, be sure they have solid support under their feet.

Cautious children and natural planners like to know what's coming. Let them practice step-by-step—pants down, sit, stand, and pants up.

Fenson Fawn got really frightened by the noisy flushes in public restrooms and he worried that he would get sucked down the toilet. Mom used toilet paper to cover the sensor above public toilets so they wouldn't flush until Fenson was ready. One day at home, she put a head-sized ball in the toilet and flushed: "Watch! The ball doesn't go down, and you won't either."

Mom often told easily frustrated Tarita Turtle, "You need to use the potty so you can go to preschool." Tarita didn't know what preschool was so she didn't want to go. Tarita thought, "If I keep using diapers, I won't have to go." Mom realized her mistake. She stopped talking about potty training and preschool together. Mom took Tarita to visit the preschool, and told her which friends would also go there.

Rewards

Creative parents find lots of rewards for potty success. Rewards will only work when the child is really ready, however.

Busy BayLee didn't want to stop and sit on the potty. Dad got him to practice by letting him watch a potty video on his I-pad. Then BayLee asked to wear superhero pants, but when he did, he always wet them. Mom put him back in pull-ups, but he took them off and peed on the carpet. So Mom put on pull-ups and his overalls backwards so he couldn't take them off. She said, "BayLee, you can wear big boy pants when you are ready to pee in the toilet. We'll try again in a few months."

Some scientific types love the fact that on the potty or toilet, they can bend over, watch the poop come out, and make it come faster or slower. Some boys love target practice—aiming at Cheerios in the toilet.

Children may earn fancy panties, time with favorite games or art supplies, or an outing after a certain number of successes. Given that potty training only happens once, it's an okay time for sweet rewards.

When training isn't in place by 4, some parents increase incentives by having the child help with clean-up. Activities that the child takes for granted might become rewards, such as trips to the park, scooter rides outside, or playdates. As in other situations, know whether you are dealing with "can't" cooperate or "won't." Check with your child's doctor.

Sibling Rivalry

Baby in Arms

Tegan Tiger is a natural planner. To prepare her for the new baby, Mom practiced things with her before the baby came home. They sat side by side and talked while Mom held a doll to her breast. Mom also said, "If you touch the baby gently, your fingernails will stay the same color. If you touch too hard, your finger nails will change to red." Mom and Tegan practiced touching each other gently.

Because BayLee is so active, his mom planned ways to use his energy around a new baby. He could run and fetch diapers and blankets. He could also be the indoor baby mover. Mom put baby BeiBei in a laundry basket so BayLee could push her around house. (Mom stayed close by for safety, and made sure there was no risk from stairs.) BayLee loved his job and didn't feel left out as he did when Mom carried the baby around.

By late afternoon, BayLee was often worn out emotionally. He was tired from a frustrating day and had trouble figuring out what to do next. He gradually figured out that if he bumped or poked BeiBei, or squeezed her hand, Mom came in a hurry! Mom would be angry, but at least she would come and tell him what to do next.

One day Mom told BayLee, "You can get my angry attention or my happy attention. If you hurt BeiBei you get my angry attention. But if you ask for a hug, or to look at a book together, or ask me to put on an exercise video, you'll get my happy attention." BayLee was surprised. He hadn't known how to get Mom's *happy* attention. Mom also looked for more ways she and BayLee could have time together. She asked him to be her special helper. He could stuff clothes in the dryer, sort socks, help make beds, wash potatoes and plastic dishes. Even though his help didn't always save time, it helped BayLee feel important so he got into less trouble. Mom and BayLee also put a picture list on the refrigerator of easy things he could do at the end of the day.

Baby Now Babbles

Around 6 months, Mom said BeiBei needed help learning to talk. She asked BayLee to slowly tell her important words and to repeat back the funny sounds she made. If Mom had to step into another room, she asked BayLee to make funny faces so BeiBei would laugh.

Baby Begins to Crawl

Now Tegan, a natural planner, had a hard time. Her brother crawled into all her projects and messed them up. Tegan hit him and pushed him away. Her parents got angry until they realized that Tegan needed space of her own. They said she could do projects on the dining room table or could play with her dolls on Mom and Dad's bed. Because her brother didn't bother her things, she was kinder to him when they played together.

Baby Toddles and Grabs Toys

Between toddling and turning 3, Tegan's little brother was a real problem. He was attracted to his older sister who had many skills he wanted to learn. He pestered her unmercifully, copying, grabbing, hitting, and biting. Mom taught Tegan to trade another toy with her brother to get back one he had taken. Mom also said, "You can hold his hand if he tries to hit you. And whenever you need help, come and tell me."

Tegan sometimes climbed into the empty playpen to get away from her brother. In time, their parents fenced off a corner of the living room so Tegan could have some safe play space. (Some older siblings are glad to retreat to their own room for peace and quiet. To more social siblings, that can feel like exile. They do better with a protected space near other family members.)

Baby Turns 3

At this point, life changed for BayLee. His parents complimented BeiBei for getting dressed all by herself and sitting quietly at the table. BeiBei got more compliments, and BayLee got more complaints. He was afraid Mom didn't love him as much as BeiBei. BayLee felt sad and jealous, which made him angry. So he teased BeiBei or took her toys or pushed her. She would hit him back. BayLee would call and report, "Mommy, she hit me." It was a relief to see Mom upset with BeiBei instead of with him. When Mom realized that she couldn't figure out how fights had started, she sent both of them to time-out in separate rooms.

This plan helped, but Mon wanted an even better solution. It has two parts. First, she got a little book with blank pages. Every night, after BeiBei was sleep, she took it down from BayLee's shelf. She sat and wrote one line: "I love you when," or "I love you because . . . " She read to him what she had written, and they put his secret book back on his shelf.

Second, when she heard screaming from another room, she no longer tried to figure out what had gone wrong. Now that BeiBei could talk, she instead asked each child in turn, "What do you want right now?" Then she asked, "What is a plan that will work for both of you?" This gave BayLee and BeiBei the practice they needed to figure out their own answers.

As the Years Go By

Spirited children generally take up more emotional space in the family. If possible, spend some time alone each week with the quiet, mellow sibling, to help the family be more balanced.

Words to Help Your Child Live
with High Curiosity

Parent

If you lovingly tell your child:

You love interesting, new things.

You don't like being bored.

It's safer to look before you leap.

Child

Your child learns to say:

I love interesting, new things.

I don't like being bored.

It's safer to look before I leap.

Words to Help Your Child Live
with an Irregular Body

Parent

If you lovingly tell your child:

You get hungry at different times of the day.

You get sleepy at different times of the day.

Child

Your child learns to say:

I get hungry at different times of the day.

I get sleepy at different times of the day.

Recommended Reading

For adults

Baby Sign Language Basics: Early Communication for Hearing Babies and Toddlers by Monta Z. Briant

The Challenging Child: Understanding, Raising and Enjoying the Five "Difficult" Types of Children by Stanley I. Greenspan and Jacqueline Salmon

The Highly Sensitive Child: Helping Our Children Thrive When the World Overwhelms Them by Elaine Aron

The Out-of-Sync Child Has Fun by Carol Kranowitz

The Secret of Toddler Sharing: Why Sharing Is Hard and How to Make It Easier by Elizabeth Crary

Try and Make Me! Simple Strategies that Turn Off the Tantrums and Create Cooperation by Ray Levy and Bill O'Hanlon

For children

Feelings for Little Children series: *When you're happy and you know it; When you're mad and you know it; When you're shy and you know it; When you're silly and you know it*

I'm Frustrated by Elizabeth Crary

I'm Mad by Elizabeth Crary

The Invisible String by Patrice Karst and Geoff Stevenson

King of the Playground by Phyllis Reynolds Naylor

Moody Cow Meditates by Kerry Lee MacLean

Self-Calming Cards [deck of cards] by Elizabeth Crary and Mits Katayama

Two Homes by Claire Masurel and Kady MacDonald Denton

The Way I Feel by Janan Cain

Wemberly Worried by Kevin Henkes

What About Me? 12 Ways to Get Your Parents' Attention (Without Hitting Your Sister) by Eileen Kennedy-Moore, illustrated by Mits Katayama

Temperament Analysis Resource

Formal temperament analysis through Dr. James Cameron's website at http://www.preventiveoz.org. Parents can compare their child's temperament with other children's. Gain insight into what is moderate or extreme.

More Helpful Books from Parenting Press

Is This a Phase?
Child Development & Parent Strategies, Birth to 6 Years
by Helen F. Neville, B.S., R.N., illustrated by Jenny Williams

This comprehensive guide to why your baby or young child behaves as she does answers many a parent's cry, "Is this a phase . . . or is it forever?" Look here for experienced advice and accurate information from a long-time pediatric advice nurse. Part 1 covers development chronologically. Part 2 is a rich, fascinating collection of topics that parents have questions about. They range from "Help—Is My Child Okay?" to "Impulse Control" to "Pets" to "Screen Time." The book also contains 65 charts and diagrams to make information immediately comprehensible without a ton of reading.

Contents

Part 1 Phase by Phase: What's Happening Now?
1. All Ages: The Work of Being a Parent
2. Birth to 3 Months: Amazing Surprise Package
3. 2 to 9 Months: Falling in Love
4. Crawling to 18 Months: Off to See the World
5. 18 Months to 3 Years: Living in the Here and Now
6. 3 Years: Mostly Sunny Skies with Some Showers
7. 4 Years: The Next Declaration of Independence
8. 5 Years: Kindergarten, Ready or Not?

Part 2 Topics Over Time: An Alphabetical Reference for Dealing with Child Development in Daily Life
Activities and Toys
Art and Artists
Attention Span: How It Grows

Bilingual Babes and Beyond
Child Care and Preschool
Communication with Signs and Sounds
Death: Helping Children Cope
Discipline: What Works Now?
Diversity: Understanding Differences
Divorce
Eating: Month after Month
continued through the alphabet to
Toilet Learning: Is It Time Yet?

Is This a Phase? . . . is an authoritative reference, carefully compiled, accurate, reliable, and just plain good reading. . . . Ms. Neville is reassuring and practical.
—Thomas Breese, M.D., University of California Medical Center, San Francisco

ISBN 978-1-884734-63-2
8.25 x 10 inches, 224 pages
$22.95 U.S.
Available from www.ipgbook.com
or your favorite bookstore

Mommy! I Have to Go Potty!

A Parent's Guide to Toilet Training, 2ⁿᵈ edition
by Jan Faull, M.Ed., and updated and expanded by Helen F. Neville, B.S., R.N.

From diapers to dry nights, this book offers a clear, step-by-step approach to toilet training. Whether your child is eager or reluctant, you will find many suggestions on how to proceed with minimal stress. The "Stories from the Bathroom" show toilet learning in action and are helpful and entertaining.

Contents
1. Is It Time Yet?
2. The Parent's Role in Potty Training
3. Places to Start
4. To Reward or Not to Reward

Helpful information and sound advice . . . I will happily refer parents to this book and will add it to the first, well-worn edition already in my lending library.
—Nancy Glass-Quattrin, R.N., Encopresis Treatment Center, Edmonds, Washington

[The authors'] common sense, websites, references, and anecdotes all merge to provide a reassuring and encouraging approach.
—Gary Spector, M.D., Seattle Children's Hospital

ISBN 978-0-9650477-1-5
5.5 x 8.5 inches, 176 pages
$14.95 U.S.
Available from www.ipgbook.com
or your favorite bookstore

What to Do About Sleep Problems in Young Children, 12 Months to 5 Years

by Helen F. Neville, B.S., R.N.
"A Parenting Press Qwik Book"

This book will help you find hope when you're tired, want rest for your cranky kids, and peace for your whole family. Sleep is a basic need. We get tired, we sleep. What could be simpler? Sometimes, though, sleep is a complicated affair. Helen F. Neville, a pediatric nurse for 30 years, has fielded more questions from parents about sleep than about any other topic. Whatever you're experiencing in your family, she has probably already proposed a strategy for it.

Contents

This short book is amazing in the quantity and quality of the author's sugges-tions on getting kids to sleep. She helped me figure out what was really going on (different from what I had thought) and then how to make a plan. If you're worn out, get this book!
—Elizabeth, mother of three under 6 years

ISBN 978-1-884734-88-5
5.5 x 8.5 inches, 32 pages
$9.95 U.S.
Available from www.ipgbook.com
or your favorite bookstore

The Biting Solution

The Expert's No-Biting Guide
for Parents, Caregivers, and Early Childhood Educators

by Lisa Poelle, M.A.

Does your child bite siblings, friends, class-mates — and you? Is your child threatened with expulsion from child care because of chronic biting? Are you a child care provider exasperat-ed with a child who won't stop biting?

Lisa Poelle has years of experience with families and early childhood programs where help is needed to cope with a youngster who bites. With *The Biting Solution* parents and caregivers can identify why kids bite, and teach them more effective ways to express themselves and to get along with others.

In this book you will find:
- a script that walks you through what to do and say the instant a child bites
- 7 questions to determine why this child bites
- what adults need to know about child development, temperament, and limit setting to prevent biting
- a puppet show script and songs that teach kids to communicate without biting, hitting, or other inappropriate behavior
- case histories that show how families and caregivers have used Poelle's methods to permanently squelch biting in as little as a week

Wow! Great book! Parents and teachers get a better understanding of why young children resort to hurting each other, plus effective, concrete ideas to prevent and respond to these problem behaviors.
—Lauren Kuehn, director, Green Hills Pre-School, Los Gatos, California

ISBN 978-1-936903-07-8
7 x 9 inches, 128 pages
$13.95 U.S.
Available from www.ipgbook.com
or your favorite bookstore

What Angry Kids Need

Parenting Your Angry Child Without Going Mad
by Jennifer Anne Brown, M.S.W. and Pam Provonsha Hopkins, M.S.W.

Angry kids need support to deal with their feelings. They also need to be taught how to manage their behavior. The authors are specialists in treating children who express their feelings intensely. They will help you understand why your child might be angry, give you a number of effective strategies to help your child, and show you how to improve the quality of life in your home.

Contents

An exceptionally well written usable book for emotional education that every parent needs! An important tool to understand, manage and appreciate the purpose of anger and the healthy expression of this valuable emotion.
—Ann Corwin, Ph.D., child and family therapist

ISBN 978-1-884734-84-7
5.5 x 8.5 inches, 144 pages
$14.95 U.S.
Available from www.ipgbook.com
or your favorite bookstore

Index

About the Authors

Helen F. Neville is a pediatric nurse, educator, and researcher at Kaiser Permanente in California. Her goad as a temperament specialist is "to take the mystery out of young children's behavior." She is also the author of Is This a Phase? Child Development & Parent Strategies, Birth to 6 Years.

Diane Clark Johnson is a certified family life educator. She was a challenging child herself and is raising another, so she really understands the kind of help parents are looking for.